Transracial Adoption, Identity, and Racism in the United States

Transracial Adoption, Identity, and Racism in the United States

Between Two Worlds

Kyrai E. Antares

LEXINGTON BOOKS
Lanham • Boulder • New York • London

Published by Lexington Books
An imprint of The Rowman & Littlefield Publishing Group, Inc.
4501 Forbes Boulevard, Suite 200, Lanham, Maryland 20706
www.rowman.com

86-90 Paul Street, London EC2A 4NE, United Kingdom

British Library Cataloguing in Publication Information Available

Library of Congress Cataloging-in-Publication Data

Names: Antares, Kyrai E., 1974- author.
Title: Transracial adoption, identity, and racism in the United States : between two worlds / Kyrai E Antares.
Description: Lanham : Lexington Books, [2023] | Includes bibliographical references and index. | Summary: "This volume contains narratives of Black transracial adoptees which illustrate the socialization experiences that directly affect their complex racial identities as emerging adults. The author argues that transracial adoption stems from systemic issues of racial injustice, and that those problems will not be solved quickly"—Provided by publisher.
Identifiers: LCCN 2023007993 (print) | LCCN 2023007994 (ebook) | ISBN 9781666914597 (cloth) | ISBN 9781666914603 (epub)
Subjects: LCSH: Interracial adoption—United States. | Adoptees—United States—Identification.
Classification: LCC HV875.64 .A58 2023 (print) | LCC HV875.64 (ebook) | DDC 362.7340973—dc23/eng/20230309
LC record available at https://lccn.loc.gov/2023007993
LC ebook record available at https://lccn.loc.gov/2023007994

For Julaeya

Contents

Preface

Becoming a parent is a life-changing experience for which one can never be fully prepared. When becoming a transracial adoptive parent, racial difference is added to the other aspects of parenting and family life. Raising children who don't look like you and who live very different experiences in the racialized United States calls for a unique skill set. Part of being prepared is to understand the context of the United States' racialized caste system or white racial frame and how that context appears in the lives of transracial adoptive families. Knowing this context is paramount in navigating the challenges of transracial adoption, white anti-racist identity development, and embracing a multiracial family experience. Unfortunately, when someone becomes a foster and/or adoptive parent, there are no systems in place to supply the needed education and training to build this foundation of knowledge and experience. My hope is that this book will be one resource of many to assist parents, adoptees, researchers, therapists, and adoption workers through experiences of transracial adoption.

In my work as a licensed psychologist, adjunct professor, and anti-racism consultant, I have seen from different positions some of the ways that transracial adoption is a unique phenomenon in which the presence of race, racism, white supremacy, and the white racial frame come into focus. Transracial adoptees commonly bear the impact of the white racial frame in transracial adoption due to the blinders firmly affixed upon those of us with racial privilege. This book intends to expand the perspective of researchers, transracial adoptive parents, and adoption professionals so that those who benefit from racial privilege can begin to help carry the burden of the inherited story of race we are all living in the United States.

While some of my experience with transracial adoption is professional and academic, I also have personal experience as a transracial adoptive parent. When I was 34, I became a single foster parent. One of the children I fostered became my forever daughter through adoption. I am White, and my daughter is multiracial. The experience of being the parent of a child who does not look like me brought my previous intellectual understanding of race, racism, and living in a racialized culture to a new and eye-opening place through experience. Suddenly I was asked intrusive questions: (a) What is she? (b) What is the father? (c) What is she mixed with? (d) Where is her real mom? (e) Where did you adopt her from? (f) What is her race? (g) What is her ethnicity? (h) Is she half Black? None of these questions had ever been asked of me when my elder child was a baby, who has the same racial identity as I do. People did not react to us with questions and curiosity about racialized categorization. Rather, we were approached with comments and questions that did not feel invasive: (a) Your baby is so cute! (b) Does he sleep through the night? (c) He looks just like you!

As my daughter grew, questions were addressed to her about being with a White parent. Children in the library, upon hearing her call me "mom" would question her, "That's your mom?" Sometimes, even after she answered affirmatively, the child would come to me and ask, "Are you really her mom?" School mates would stop my older child in the hall to ask if his sister was adopted. Eventually, he came to the pat answer: "Does it matter?"

The constant curiosity about my daughter and our family became a daily part of our lives—and it continues to be so. Only in a society where race and racialization are paramount would such questions be so commonplace. I have often wondered if people ever consider what message they are sending to my daughter by interrogating whether and how she belongs in her family.

Interestingly, the inquiries we receive are very different in emotional tone depending on the race of the person asking. When White adults ask, "What is she?" it feels almost as if they are looking for a receptacle for a set of assumptions based in the racialized caste system at the ready and would like to know which stereotypes to apply to the situation. People of color, Black people in particular, usually ask the question, "What is she mixed with?" This just feels different. My daughter and I have discussed that it feels more like Black people are extending a welcome or inquiring to know if she should be claimed as racial family. A closeness comes from the conversation, whereas with the previously described situation, increased distance is the result.

Another important aspect of my life that led me to writing this book is my anti-racist identity development process. My journey related to recognizing and understanding whiteness began when I was 18 years old with experiences I had during my first year of college with my group of friends, who were Black. One afternoon, two admissions administrators called me into their office and informed me that I should be more careful when choosing friends. They said people were going to get the wrong idea about me if I stayed in "that circle of people." I saw how unsurprised my friends were when I told them about this incident. I witnessed fist fights because of the n-word being used as a weapon by White football players. When several race-related fights broke out during athletic events, I saw all of the Black students on campus move into one wing of a dorm in solidarity and for safety in numbers. I learned about a world from which I had been insulated. In the three decades that have followed those initial experiences, there has been generous culture sharing on the part of my friends, open conversations about race and how we were raised to think about it, and a bridging of racial worlds that resulted in lifelong friendships.

Moving to Berea, Kentucky brought a community aspect to my journey through conversations with women who attended Berea College and had an interest in studies of privilege and oppression. Prior to these conversations, my learning had been experiential. Being in the Berea community lent language to my development. While living in Berea, my White identity became much more real to me with the experience of fostering and adopting transracially. My awareness of the racial privilege I carry became clearer. I saw firsthand how I did not have to explain my origins, I never had to worry about being questioned about my appearance, and the social world here in the United States was made for people who look like me. At this time, I was still convinced that if I knew enough and always did the right thing, I could avoid "being racist."

In my late thirties, entering the doctoral program at Western Michigan University deepened and expanded my White racial identity journey by adding the *anti-racist* identity to the mix. I encountered professors and colleagues who were continuously pushing themselves and others to go further on the path and to be a part of a movement to dismantle systems of privilege in education and in society. I was required to reflect on and discuss the ways my whiteness was a factor in interactions, both personally and professionally. I began to not only be more aware of my racial privilege and how I unconsciously participate in this country's system of racism, but I found ways to use the racial privilege I have to make change. I was encouraged to study, read, write, and present on topics related to race, racism and privilege, and I was able to incorporate these topics into my teaching assistant position in the education department. In addition, living in a mostly Black neighborhood while in Michigan was an important aspect of racial identity development for me and my children.

These experiences combined to form the motivation and interest in conducting a qualitative study focused on transracial adoption for my doctoral dissertation. I consulted with professors and poured over the research on transracial adoption to see if there was a worthwhile contribution I could make to the field. I considered several different study topics and designs. In the end, I decided that there was a lot of work to be done to bring the narratives of adoptees to the front of the field of transracial adoption. A phenomenological study works to tell the stories of those interviewed from their perspective, preserving their narratives as the informing agent for consumers of the literature. I chose to focus my research on the voices of adoptees so that their stories could be the motivation and guide for change.

Because my ever-growing lens has developed to the point of seeing racialized dynamics in all aspects of my daily life, I believe there is no person, situation, or place in this country that is not impacted by race and racism. As my daughter grows into an adolescent, our journey as a multiracial family continues. Race is a daily topic of conversation for all of us. We discuss differences in our racial identities, observe and analyze our experiences in the world and how they are unique, and we remain dedicated to growing our multiracial anti-racist family identity. We read books about anti-racism and the history of race in our country. We watch relevant movies, and pause them to talk about what we are watching. When my daughter comes home with stories from school where she calls out microaggressions or stereotyping or experiences being treated differently due to race, we talk about it and process what happened. We also connect to community resources, media and music, counseling and mentorship professionals, friends, and neighbors in our commitment to connect my daughter to experiences that affirm her racial identity and to further the white anti-racist identity development of White family members. The choices we make as a family and the choices I make as a parent are rooted in a commitment to continue my journey of anti-racist identity development. Doing these things takes work, creativity, and openness. I make mistakes, and I know that will always happen because of the insidiousness of white supremacy. I don't expect to be perfect, but I do expect to remain committed and to continue taking actions that affirm and value her existence.

During this research project, I knew my story of adoption would enhance my empathy with participants and develop a point of identification that helped build rapport. However, it was vital that I recognized that each adoptive parent and each adoptee is a unique person with a unique perspective. Not every parent noticed or minded the questions that, to me, were extremely invasive and indicative of systemic racism. Not every adoptee felt "othered" by such inquiries. My family's story served as an inspiration for this project, but it was not used as a model by which my participants' stories were shaped.

This book is an invitation. To transracial adoptive parents, it is an invitation to enter into a deeper connection to your child as a whole person, including racial identity and experiences related to race. It is an invitation to embrace the unknown and find that when we let go of who we thought we were, we make room for who we never even imagined we could become. It is an encouragement to do *more* work when you feel uncomfortable, ask *more* questions when you feel exposed, and bring humility to this process which is meant to humanize you. To educators, social workers, psychologists, and counselors, this is an invitation to consider the narratives of nine emerging adults who shared thematic aspects of an experience that is often unnoticed, undiscussed, unnamed, unaddressed and unsolved: Black children being raised by white people who are mostly not committed to anti-racism in themselves, their families, or their communities. In our work with transracial adoptees as clients, we have a duty to listen to their stories intently and to remember that we can play a role in making the transracial adoption experience different for coming generations.

Most importantly, this book is meant to provide transracial adoptees with access to a community of people who have lived through similar, even though not identical, circumstances. Regardless of the differences in specific situations, shared themes emerged when transracial adoptees discussed their experiences related to race. My hope is that other transracial adoptees will read these chapters and feel less alone.

Acknowledgments

I would like to acknowledge the generosity, authenticity and willingness of the nine people who served as participants in the research study that made this book possible. I am forever grateful to these nine people for trusting me to tell their stories, even while aware of how my profession has historically exploited Black people. Your patience with me and the research process, your willingness to make time for interviews and journal entries, and your honest feedback along the way has made this study incredibly meaningful and genuine. Thank you.

Thank you to Rhonda M. Roorda for kindly providing consultation about the publishing aspect of this project. Your work is an inspiration!

Thank you to Amy Zitzelberger, for generously contributing time and skill to editing this book, for community in adoption, and for your friendship over all these years. Thank you to Rosanne and Christy O'Connor, for being the best god family to Laeya and for helping me have quiet time to write. Thank you to Tonya Pierson and Camille Collins for opening your hearts and home to Laeya, which has helped her in more ways than you know. Thank you, Cassi Parsley, for being there for Laeya as a sister, an influence, and a loving presence. Thank you, Dr. Dawnielle Simmons, for your influence on Laeya, and for your continued support in authentic living and remaining ever-vigilant about white supremacy. Thank you to my friends and family for your encouragement and love, and for being forever family to Laeya: Adarsa Antares, Dawn Branch, Ryan Cook, Jewel Willard, Doreen Crispino Parsley, Riley Vandelinder, Jackson Vandelinder, Jordan Vandelinder, the Dixon Family, my Berea family, Carrie MacGillis, Kaylie MacGillis, Christine and Kevin Thompson.

Thank you to my children, Dmitri Rose and Laeya Antares, who fill my heart and home with love and endless inspiration.

Introduction

In 2020, Netflix released the limited series called *Colin in Black and White*, a retelling of Colin Kaepernick's adolescent and teenage years growing up in a transracially adoptive home. This film provides glimpses into the close connection between the systemic dynamics of White supremacy and racism and the interpersonal familial dynamics of a transracial adoptive home. There is a quality to Colin's home that can be seen as reflective of systemic dynamics of racism, and wherein Colin was left to traverse the terrain of being a Black teenager in an environment rooted in denial of issues of race, the unnamed White privilege of Colin's parents, and isolation in the experience of blackness. Colin's White parents both loved and supported him but also did not notice when issues of race were weighing heavily on their son, when he was being treated differently due to his race, and how they perpetuated White supremacy in their home even while being "good people."

How different might Colin Kaepernick's upbringing have been if he had been able to talk with his White parents about race? What if they had made sure he saw people who looked like him regularly, if their friend group had been diverse, if they had lived in a neighborhood with racial diversity, if his mother had continued to get his hair done properly and learned to care for it, if race and racism could have been openly discussed, and if his parents had been committed to an anti-racist journey? Colin would still have experienced the same racism, but it would have been in a different family context—one much less isolated, confusing, and unspoken. With a family at home that welcomed these conversations and found personal relevance in them, Colin would have been able to develop language and conceptual understandings that would help him build his own identity as he grew up. The experience shown in *Colin in Black and White* is one person's life experience, but it is representative of an often-overlooked narrative of Black people being raised in White adoptive homes in the United States. Interestingly, race-focused awareness and skills training for transracially adopting parents is not required. Vonk and Angaran (2002) found that less than half of adoption agencies in their study offered any multicultural training, and it was unclear whether the trainings that were offered included information specifically about race. In fact, widely accepted interpretations of the Multiethnic Placement Acts (passed in 1994 and amended in 1996) assert that requiring race-focused training would be in violation of the law, because the act prohibits the consideration of a child's race, ethnicity or national origin in foster and adoptive placements (McRoy & Griffin, 2012).

Due to lack of training and the largely unconscious nature of White racial socialization, racial socialization practices of White parents with Black children are, by default, largely derived from familial and systemically informed belief systems of the parents. Parents serve as interpreters of the social structure in which the family lives and provide a buffer between children and the society (Taylor & Thornton, 1996). The interpretation of social structure by White parents is, by default, rooted in whiteness. Whiteness is a position in society that includes unearned structural advantage (Twine & Steinbugler, 2006). In other words, whiteness is the lens through which White people are conditioned to see the world.

For a transracially adopted child, the formative years spent with the family are the main influence on development. Therefore, the chosen parenting paradigm and racial communication approach have a significant influence on how a Black transracially adopted child meets the world and sees themselves in the world. Parental attitudes about and attention to their adopted child's racial and cultural identity has a direct influence on the identity development process for adoptees. Research has shown that White people who adopt transracially, both domestically and internationally, most often raise their children in predominantly White spaces (Barn, 2012; Lee, 2003; Smith, Jacobson, & Juarez, 2011), much like Colin Kaepernick's parents did. Therefore, it is important to investigate how living in predominantly White environments and receiving race lessons from White parents (and important others, e.g., teachers, religious leaders) might influence transracial adoptees into adulthood, as they leave the protective buffers of the White nuclear adoptive family of their childhood (Raible, 2006).

Because an emerging adult faces a greater level of independence, which includes more unprotected interaction with the adult world, the voices of Black emerging adult transracial adoptees provide a picture of the perspective that grows from being a Black emerging adult who was raised by White parents. In addition, there are very few studies that investigate transracially adopted adults' retrospective views of their childhood in terms of preparation for the racialized world to be experienced in adulthood. Raible (2006) calls for such research, noting that adoptees are often conceptualized as perpetual children, and that considering how adult adoptees are experiencing race is vital.

This book shares the narratives of nine young adults who are Black and were raised by White families in the Midwestern region of the United States of America. Adoptees were asked to provide pseudonyms to be used in this publication for identity protection. Their descriptions of their lives, families, selves, and racial socialization experiences provide a view into the complexities of transracial adoption and also help to illustrate the commonalities and differences among transracial adoptive experiences. Memories and stories of growing up years are shared by the adoptees, as well as reflections on life in young adulthood and what it is like to be living in the current racial climate of the United States as Black people who were raised in White families. The qualitative nature of this book seeks to bring the voices of adoptees into the forefront. Their narratives inform a more complete understanding of the transracial adoptive experience. A deeper understanding of transracial adoptees' experiences is potentially beneficial to adoptees directly by giving accurate voice to this unique experience, and indirectly by providing descriptions through which social workers, psychologists, policy makers, and adoptive parents could gain knowledge to serve this population better.

CHAPTER OVERVIEW

In chapter 1, "Transracial Adoption in America," I will provide the necessary historical setting, psychological background, and social context needed to understand the importance of increasing the focus on hearing the narratives of transracial adoptees to inform improvement in the practices of transracial adoptive parents and adoption professionals. Chapters 2 through 7 of this book are composed of transracial adoptee narratives from interviews and digital journal entries. Voices of participants who are Black transracial adoptees form the bulk of these chapters. Chapter 2, "Growing up Transracially Adopted: Memories and Reflections," gives insight into which experiences related to race were formative for these adoptees during childhood. Included are stories related to identity, the importance of race, experiencing racism, representation, expectations, and communication with family members. Chapter 3, "Between Two Worlds," highlights narratives from early adulthood for adoptees, including stories about friendships, dating, feeling disconnected from Black culture, and embracing blackness. In chapter 4, "Growth in Black Identity," readers will find aspects of participant narratives focused on a growth in Black identity, those times in emerging adulthood during which adoptees felt their sense of being a Black person increasing in importance and fullness. Moving into chapter 5, "Views of Family Related to Race," the focus shifts toward how participants experience family relationships related to race during emerging adulthood. This chapter includes experiences of having to teach family, as well as stories of loyalty, allegiance and gratitude. In chapter 6, "The Political is Personal," participants share about their investment in understanding dynamics of oppression and privilege, and their personal experiences of racial politics becoming relevant in their lives. Included are stories of realizing the relevance of racial politics in adoptee's lives, as well as racial divide within families. In chapter 7, "This is Me," adoptees share their understandings of who they are at this point in their lives, the ways they see what they needed and didn't get from parents, and how their unique identities as transracial adoptees shape their perspective on self and the world.

In chapter 8, "Transracial Adoption and the White Racial Frame," the content of adoptee narratives described in the chapters 2 through 7 is discussed through the theoretical lens of the white racial frame. This chapter connects the white racial frame to specific life content of adoptees, helping to make visible the very present, even if unintentional, dynamics of systemic racism and racialized identities within transracial adoption. Chapter 9, "Transracial Adoptive Parenting," addresses preparation provided by parents to adoptees, specific recommendations for transracial adoptive parents, and explanations of parenting paradigms with adoptee narrative examples. Chapter 10, "A Note to Research, Adoption, and Counseling Professionals," offers input on directions forward for professionals in transracial adoption, including researchers, policy makers, adoption workers, and counseling psychologists. The intention of this chapter is to show how the adoptee narratives shared in this book can influence the ways in which transracial adoption is researched, conceptualized and practiced moving forward.

The intention of this book project is to give Black transracially adopted emerging adults a forum through which to contemplate and share their stories of experiencing and understanding race, their memories of racial socialization, and their feelings of preparedness for living in a racialized society as Black people after being raised by White parents. The importance of this study is evidenced by the authenticity, genuineness, and vulnerability with which these nine participants shared their experiences through interviews and journal entries. My hope is that this research effort, composed of their narratives, will inspire a much-needed change in racial literacy on the part of all professionals who work with people touched by transracial adoption. With greater awareness and training based on the needs of adoptees, systems can gradually change to encourage truly multiracial families with parents aware of race and adopted children who grow into adults who don't feel stuck between two worlds but instead feel at home in their own skin, steeped in the familial, cultural, and social support they need.

PARTICIPANTS

Nine people participated in the qualitative study that invited the narratives that form this book. Each participant met the following inclusion criteria: Black/African American or Biracial with Black parentage racial identity, transracially adopted and raised by White parents, placed with adoptive parents prior to age five, raised in Michigan, Ohio, or Indiana, and age 18–28 at the time of interviews and journal entries. See Table 0.1 for information on age, racial identity, gender and sexual orientation. Participants' personal descriptive terms were used in Table 0.1 in order to maintain alignment with the intention to keep participant voices at the forefront of this book. The reason for a narrow geographical focus is that racial socialization and experiences around race may differ across regions of the United States. The experience of transracial adoption in the Midwest region of the US might differ from the experience of transracial adoption in the South, West, Northwest, or Northeast. The intention of this study is to begin a specific line of research making comparisons among experiences possible by first clearly describing each unique experience. Four participants identified as Black, three as African American, one as Biracial: Black and White, and one as Multiracial: African American and Caucasian.

Three participants grew up in Michigan, and six were raised in Ohio. Gender identities were reported as follows: one cisgender male, one cisgender female, five female, one woman, and one male. In terms of sexual orientation, two participants identified as queer, one as bisexual, and six as heterosexual. Ages of participants spanned the full 18–28 range at the time of interviews and journal entries. This cohort of transracial adoptees were born between the years of 1982 or 1983 and 1999 or 2000. Technically, this would place the target population in the category of "Millennials," who are those born between 1980 and 2000 and are the first generation to come of age

Table 0.1 Participant Demographic Information.

Participant	*Age*	*Racial Identity*	*Gender Identity*	*Sexual Orientation*
Sadie	19	African American	Female	Heterosexual
Simone	21	African American	Female	Straight
Cherise	20	Black	Woman	Queer
Alyson	27	Black	Cisgender Female	Heterosexual
Emilie	24	Biracial (B&W)	Female	Straight
Jacob	18	Biracial (B&W)	Male	Heterosexual
Austin	28	Black	Cisgender Male	Queer
Maryama	21	African American	Female	Bisexual
Kaitlyn	18	Black	Female	Heterosexual

Note: All identifying terms in table are terms provided by participants

in the new millennium (Pew Research Center, 2017). All participants were placed with their adoptive parents at age two or younger, with most being placed within the first months of life. The age of placement was considered important because children under five have fewer permanent memories of cultural influences associated with race. Socioeconomic background information was reported as well. One participant reported being from an upper-class background, five participants reported being from a middle/upper class background, one participant from a middle-class background, one from a lower/middle class background, and one from a low-income background. Socioeconomic factors were spontaneously discussed by participants during interviews and in journal entries, which made this layer of the textured experience of transracial adoption relevant to include.

An expanded discussion of key concepts (Race, Racialization, Ethnicity, Culture, Systemic Racism, White Racial Frame) and an explanation of the author's use of these terms is provided in Appendix B.

Chapter 1

Transracial Adoption in the United States

Transracial adoption (TRA) has been a controversial issue in the United States for many decades (Barn, 2012; Feigelman, 2000). Transracial adoption occurs when infants or children are adopted by parents of a different race (Baden & Steward, 2007a). It is estimated that 2.5 percent of households in the United States include adopted children (Samuels, 2009; Smith et al., 2011), and approximately 40 percent of those adoptions are transracial (Leslie, Smith, & Hrapczynski, 2013). Domestic transracial adoption describes adoptions that take place within a country, whereas international adoption refers to those that occur between countries. According to the National Survey of Adopted Parents (NSAP), an estimated 54.5 percent of transracial adoptions are international, with the remaining split between approximately 25 percent domestic transracial adoptions from the foster care system, and 20 percent private domestic transracial adoptions (Smith et al., 2011). In the United States, while Black youth comprise 13.4 percent of the population, Black youth comprise 23 percent of children in foster care (Children's Bureau, 2021).

This book focuses on Black emerging adults who were adopted and raised by White parents. Viewing transracial adoption within the context of the *white racial frame* (an old and continuing racial framing of US society) and systemic racism, the controversy about transracial adoption can be seen as a byproduct of a systemically racist society. To see the systemic context, White people must engage in a critical examination of the racially oppressive society created by ancestors and perpetuated into contemporary times (Feagin, 2010). Because of the unique, historically rooted, dehumanizing racial framing of Black Americans that began with the enslavement of African people for labor in the North American colonies, the modern-day experiences of Black Americans are tied to that specific history and the framing used to justify slavery. Likewise, the modern-day experiences of White Americans are tied to the specific history and framing of White people as the "owners" of other human beings. Because of these unique historical facts, Black transracial adoptees should be considered as a unique population, and not grouped with other racial minorities. While all racial minorities are positioned below White people on the racial hierarchy in the United States, the Black experience in America is not the same as the Indigenous American, Latinx, Asian American, or Arab American experience. One can see that the disproportionate number of Black children in the foster care system awaiting adoption (Donaldson Adoption Institute, 2008; Lee, 2003) and the lack of recruitment of Black adoptive families (Donaldson Adoption Institute, 2008; McRoy & Griffin, 2012). Also, most foster care workers in charge of decisions about child removal and family preservation are White women (Barn, 2012). These facts reflect the racialized power differential that weaves through all United States institutions.

Even though transracial adoption has been controversial, it will likely continue for some time due to the disproportionate number of children of color in the foster care system and the systemic division of resources placing White parents in a position in which adoption is more financially feasible. While working to raise awareness of those systemic issues to decrease the rate of transracial adoption, transracial adoptees will benefit from increasing interventions and guidance to raise consciousness and skills in White parents, encouraging and equipping professionals working with transracial foster and adoptive families, and bringing growth in racial awareness to the center of transracial adoptive homes.

Due to societal history related to race in the United States, people face continued psychological, emotional, and practical results of that history. Transracial adoption brings the complexities of wider societal race relations into a family on both conscious and unconscious levels. The racial socialization that happens subtly and overtly in transracial adoptive families shows up in everyday life, blending with daily interactions and experiences. Feagin (2011) points to the presence of what he terms the white racial frame in transracial adoptive parenting. He states that the parents interviewed in a 2011 study of transracial adoptive parents (Smith et al., 2011) regularly think, act, and interact out of the *white racial frame*. For example, the parents interviewed spoke of discrimination and racism only as personal prejudice, excluding the recognition of the reality of racial oppression as institutionalized and foundational in the United States (Feagin). Smith et al. (2011) point specifically to race lessons from White parents that are rooted in the *white racial frame* and perpetuate white supremacy.

The absence of formal training specifically focused on race is a salient issue in transracial adoption because White parents do not, by default, have the experiential instruction that comes with living with daily racism and discrimination (Raible, 2006; Vonk, 2001). In addition, White parents have the choice, due to their racially privileged status, whether to grow in racial awareness and racial identity (Taylor & Thorton, 1996). White parents are largely unexposed to diverse perspectives (Raible, 2006). Research suggests that transracial adoptees tend to grow up in predominantly White environments, and rarely have interracial contact (Langrehr, Thomas, & Morgan, 2016; Smith et al., 2011). A consistent aspect of racial socialization found in research focused on Black families is preparation for bias (Hughes, Rodriguez, Smith, Johnson, Stevenson, & Spicer, 2006). Black families dealing with discrimination on a daily basis understand the importance of preparing their children for the world in which they will live. Without this aspect of racial socialization, transracially adopted children of color may reach adulthood still unprepared, psychologically and emotionally, to handle the realities they will inevitably face as people of color in the US (Raible, 2006).

Being adopted further complicates the already challenging process of development in terms of identity, adjustment, and feelings of belonging for Black children in the United States (Baden & Steward, 2007a). Differences and similarities with members of both the adoptive and the birth family are a common preoccupation for adoptees, even when racial differences are not present (Grotevant et al., 2000). Coming to terms with oneself in the context of both family and culture are primary tasks in the adoptive identity development process, and these tasks are complicated by the social contexts of the white racial frame and systemic racism. Added to the task of developing an identity as an adopted person is the task of adapting to one's status within the context of an oppressive dominant culture (Grotevant, 1997).

One argument against transracial adoption is the concern that adjustment for adoptees is hindered by the unique transracial adoptive situation. In response to this concern, several studies were conducted and found that adjustment for Black transracial adoptees is quite similar to adjustment for same-race adoptees (Feigelman 2000; Shireman and Johnson, 1986; Vroegh, 1997). In these studies examining adjustment for Black transracially adopted children and adolescents, *race was not a primary topic of exploration.* Rather, self-esteem and behavioral outcomes were the focus. Considering that race was the primary reason for the comparison between transracially and same-race adopted children, this choice suggests that perhaps focus was on the positive rather than challenging aspects of transracial adoption to "prove" that it is a benign experience for adoptees. This research may have been helpful in encouraging permanence for children of color by supporting transracial adoptions, but it was only a partial picture of adjustment for adoptees.

Adoption Policy also helps to describe the context of transracial adoption in the United States. The Multiethnic Placement Act (passed in 1994 and amended in 1996) prohibits the consideration of a child's race, ethnicity or national origin in foster and adoptive placements (McRoy & Griffin, 2012).

The intent of this act was to remove barriers for permanence, but this was a solution rooted deeply in a colorblind perspective that has affected transracial adoption in other ways. Widely accepted interpretations of the Multiethnic Placement Act assert that requiring race-focused training would be in violation of the law. This act follows the tradition of the Fourteenth Amendment, which does not allow racial classifications to be used unless strong public policy reasons can be given to support such classifications (Park & Green, 2000). According to those making decisions related to adoption law, such strong public policy reasons do not yet exist. This stance is in opposition to the National Association of Black Social Workers, as well as many scholars of transracial adoption issues (Park & Green, 2000; Samuels, 2009).

There has been criticism of transracial adoption research that followed the Multiethnic Placement Act. For example, some studies interview parents to learn about the adjustment of their children, rather than interviewing the children themselves (Lee, 2003). In addition, many different constructs are being examined in order to measure adjustment (Lee, 2003). Self-esteem (an individual characteristic) is often measured in quantitative studies, but there is rarely any examination of *group identity*, which is a salient aspect of living as a racial minority (Taylor & Thornton, 1996). In addition, international and domestic transracial adoptions are often combined in samples (Lee, 2003). Lee (2003) calls for researchers in transracial adoption to shift the focus away from adoptees being passive recipients of racial socialization, and toward thinking of adoptees as active change agents regarding their lives and their understanding of race and racial identity.

The importance of turning directly to the narratives of adoptees to gain understanding of the transracial adoptive experience becomes increasingly clear as details of past research are examined. In addition, the white racial frame (Feagin, 2010, 2013) in the United States makes it especially important for voices of participants to be kept primary throughout research focused on participants who are racial minorities. The study from which the stories in this book originate utilized both interviews with participants and journal entries from participants about their experiences related to race. Names of participants featured in this book have been changed to their chosen pseudonym. The method of research employed was hermeneutic phenomenology. This method seeks to understand the meaning of a phenomenon *as the participants experience it* (Finlay, 2014), and it is particularly useful as a method of research meant to serve the interests of oppressed populations. Orbe (2000) asserts that phenomenological inquiry is well-designed for research related to issues of race/ethnicity by providing multidimensional descriptions. Transracial adoption, being raised by White parents, and experiences of emerging adulthood related to race are all conducive to such multidimensional descriptions. In response to the deficits of previous transracial adoption research, my intention was to keep the narratives of adoptees at the forefront of this work, positioned to inform progressive, adoptee-centered change in transracial adoption.

Chapter 2

Growing Up Transracially Adopted

Memories and Reflections

No experience is comparable to growing up transracially adopted in the United States. In this chapter, transracial adoptees share reflections of their growing up years. An awareness of the importance of race began at a young age for many participants. Participants tell stories of events when they became aware of race, reflect on what it was like to be a different race than parents and other family members, and share thoughts and feelings while looking back on the experience.

Maryama and Jacob shared specific stories about becoming aware of race during childhood. Maryama tells of a time when her belonging to her mother was questioned by a classmate:

> I can remember the very first time where race became a factor in my life. I was very young, kindergarten actually, where I remember having show-and-tell. I was so excited because it was my day to show and my mom was bringing in our new puppy. When my mom had finally arrived, she walked through the door and at that very moment I was filled with joy and excitement, not only because my dog was there but because I got to see my mom in school. One of my really good friends at the time came up to me and asked, "That's your mom?" as if there was something wrong. I just remember looking at him like, "Why? Of course, that's my mom! What do you mean?" The kid had a blank look on his face, and he said, "But she's White and you're Black."

While she might not have understood what it meant, this example from Maryama's journal entry illustrates her first awareness of something noticeable and socially important about her being Black and her mother being White. Similarly, one of Jacob's journal entries included a story of being a young child and realizing he was a different race than his family, but in his example, he pointed out the difference rather than a peer:

> I remember swimming in the lake and having an epiphany about myself in relation to my family. I got out of the lake, rushed over to my aunt who was talking with my dad. I pointed to my palm, and said something along the lines of, 'Dad, Aunt [de-identified], look, look! I found my White, I found my White!' My aunt responded by pointing at my heart with something along the lines of, 'Color doesn't matter, it's what is in here.' I believe that I responded with something along the lines of, 'Oh, I know, but I'm different than you. I'm Black and you're White.'

This story illustrates the dawn of Jacob's awareness of racial difference in his family, and, even when his family member responded with a "colorblind" philosophical explanation of color not mattering, he was insistent to again point to the fact that there was a difference, and he noticed it. A qualitative study conducted by Wilkerson (2014) included focus groups with 17 White parents of White children attending a racially and socioeconomically diverse school. Every parent advocated a colorblind philosophy, and wanted to teach their children to see *people* instead of race. Jacob's story is a reminder that even when raising Black children, White parents generally still rely on a colorblind approach to the topic of race.

Several participants reflected on and shared memories of moments when familial racial difference created a feeling of discomfort. Sadie shares about her feelings related to going to her White grandparents' cottage by a lake in a small rural town:

> I used to be uncomfortable going to places around there especially because of what I looked like. I know a lot of the times people around there like my grandparents' friends they always kind of looked a certain way or might have snickered to each other or something. It became noticeable. It used to make me self-conscious, and I think that's why I stopped going. I think that's kind of when I started to push that side of me away. Because in high school I think it was to the point to where I almost wished I was White.

This vignette captures the discomfort Sadie felt due to race, and it was echoed by Cherise as she described her feelings when she would encounter Black people while with her White family or friends. She stated:

> Growing up, I was kind of uncomfortable around Black people, and I didn't know how to act around them. I remember when I'd go to a salon it was mostly black women and I would be sweating sitting there. I would just feel super uncomfortable. I would think, 'Oh, are they judging me? Are they thinking I

talk a certain way? Are they judging me for being with a bunch of White people or my White friends?'

While fears related to an imaginary audience are common during adolescence, this discomfort is specifically related to racial difference and having been transracially adopted. Cherise's reflection echoes a study in which DeBerry, Scarr, and Weinberg (1996) found that Black transracially adopted children raised in White communities struggled with discomfort with their appearance and with interactions with other Black people. Alyson shares her experience of this discomfort at the age of seven:

> When I was with my family at home, I never felt abnormal or that our heterogeneous family was atypical. But the moment we stepped into public spaces it was palpable that we were different and from an early age I became paranoid of this fact. From even the age of 7 in 2nd grade, I remember feeling at ease that my mom worked in the school and everyone knew her, but they didn't know my dad. I remember that a girl a grade below me had a White mom, and a very Black dad and she was my color, so I thought, 'If they never meet my dad, maybe everyone will assume he is Black and thus not think I am weird or look confused or start to ask questions that I don't want to explain.'

Sadie, Cherise, and Alyson all describe discomfort and worried about being noticed, judged, or questioned during childhood.

Being transracially adopted requires handling the dynamics of race and racial difference while embodying a racial identity different from that of parents. Kaitlyn shared, "I was confused when I was little because I knew I was adopted, but I would still wonder why my parents were a different skin color than me." Another participant, Austin, commented on how being transracially adopted is different than same-race adoption with the statement: "Being transracially adopted, there was no hiding it, ever. There are those stories about kids who don't find out they're adopted until they're in their twenties. There was no hiding it. And so always being aware of the effect of the fact that you're adopted, whether you wanted to be or not."

EXPOSURE AND REPRESENTATION

In addition to noticing racial difference, participants also describe the amount of racial diversity in their neighborhoods and schools. Participants comment on the lack of exposure to racial diversity and/or representation of people with a shared racial identity during childhood.

Seven out of nine participants shared that lack of personal exposure and representation in media was an essential component of their experience related to race during childhood. When asked if he had much interaction with Black people, Jacob responded, "No. Little to none, actually. I've gone to private schools for most of my life, and I've really only been around Caucasian students." Austin also attended schools with few students of color. He stated, "I think there was five people that were Black that I graduated with, if that. And that was in my grade, but we were a class of 300." Reflecting on her environment growing up, Emilie shared, "I honestly can't, besides my family unit, I cannot think of any other Black people that lived in my entire neighborhood, like, just offhand." Similarly, Simone shared, "Growing up, I didn't have many friends who looked like me. My town didn't have many African Americans in it." Maryama shared a similar picture of racial diversity in her environment: "If I went to my dad's work, I would see some friends of color of his, but besides that, no. We went to an all-White church. Actually, I'm thinking of it now. My mom didn't have any African-American friends."

Cherise noticed the lack of exposure to people of color in terms of representation. She stated, "Growing up I had no Black representation. All my idols and obsessions looked nothing like me." On this same topic of representation, Alyson said her grandmother reminded her about a moment from when she was four or five years old. Alyson told her grandmother, "I wish my skin was light like yours." Alyson, hearing this story, described the following reaction:

> When my grandma told me this, I viscerally felt so sick and sad for my past self. For a 5-year-old to recognize those differences and consciously say out loud that she wanted the White skin is so telling of the subconscious messages we receive about racial hierarchy from a young age. My 5-year-old self knew nothing about race, yet my environment engrained in me that it must be better or more desirable to be White. My entire family is White. Every teacher I had was White. Every doctor I had was a White, elderly man. Every person of authority in my life was White. The majority of children in my Catholic grade school were White, with the exception of a few Asian children and around 10 Black children in grades K-8. My priest and every single human in the congregation was White. Every TV show at that age that I watched had White people or cartoon characters. Every book that was read to me had White people. One could venture to think, that as a 5-year-old, the subconscious feeling of not feeling like I belonged would resonate with me and have dire consequences all throughout my childhood and into my teens and young adulthood. And it did.

This story shows how even later in life as a young adult, Alyson saw the complexity of her experience related to race as a transracially adopted child and believed that the lack of exposure to and representation of Black people in her life had a lasting impact.

These stories about being raised in mostly White environments are in alignment with previous literature focused on transracial adoption. In a longitudinal study by Shireman and Johnson (1987), all but two of the 42 Black children being raised by White parents lived in all White neighborhoods. Parents reported that while they understood their child's need for contact with Black people, they were not willing to alter their lifestyle to make that happen.

Kaitlyn had a different experience than other participants, and grew up in a diverse town. She stated, "We had people from all races and all religions that went to school with us. So, it wasn't that difficult." Kaitlyn is the only participant who reported growing up in a racially diverse area and attending a racially diverse school. The added exposure to a diverse racial community produced opportunities for her to have casual and consistent daily contact with people of color, to be involved in conversations about race with peers, and to experience things like stereotype threat and unequal treatment at school. These events were essential in shaping her understanding of systemic inequalities based on race.

Kaitlyn's experience reflects earlier findings on transracial adoption where a diverse racial composition of neighborhoods assists children in identity development. In Simon and Alstein's (1996) longitudinal study that followed transracial adoptive families over 20 years, a respondent stated that her parent's choice to raise her in an integrated neighborhood contributed to her becoming fully comfortable with her identity.

One seminal study on the experiences of TRA was focused exclusively on domestic adoption. McRoy and Zurcher (1983) conducted a mixed methods investigation into the perceptions of and attitudes toward racial identity in 30 domestic transracial adoptive families and 30 domestic same-race adoptive families. The theoretical base for their study was symbolic interaction theory, "which assumes a person's self-definition develops from interpersonal relations in a social world" (p. 16). Their study showed that TRA children raised in mixed neighborhoods by parents with a Multiracial Orientation had sustained and frequent contact with other Black families, felt more positive about their racial identity, and were less likely to hold to White-oriented attitudes and behaviors. This result was found in Feigelman's (2000) study as well, which included results that showed TRA children expressed less discomfort related to their appearance when they lived in a racially diverse neighborhood. Similarly, in the current study, exposure and representation during childhood was discussed by all participants as an important aspect of growing up transracially adopted.

SEEING BLACK AND WHITE

This section presents how participants see the meaning behind racialized identities during childhood. They describe wrestling with stereotypical ideas related to Black people. They describe how identity fits into their understanding, seeing and experiencing privilege and oppression, and how they noticed differences in how Black and White people were treated and characterized. This section dives into the reflections participants have about the ways they were perceiving race in the world and the meaning behind their perceptions.

Sadie described her ideas about Black people when she was growing up and related those ideas to her feelings of exposure. She stated:

> I wasn't exposed to Black culture before college, and to be honest, I kind of liked it that way. As bad as it might sound to say it, I always identified myself as mixed when someone asked my race. I was proud of my White side because the encounters I did have with Black people were not very good ones. I thought they were "ghetto" and in general had less manners and consideration for others, which is what I did not want to be. In a way you could say I had preconceptions about Black people.

Echoing this idea of having preconceived ideas about Black people, Cherise shared, "Because I wasn't around a lot of Black people, I think there were times when I did view Black people in a derogatory way, like in a stereotypical way. And it's not something that I'm proud of. I don't really talk about it." Relatedly, Alyson shared her thoughts on how she thought about Black people when she was growing up:

> Back then, the way that I thought about Black people globally was that those are the people that are downtown that mostly make up the people who are homeless or begging for money; that they live downtown in the hood and that's basically what they do. That was my context for so long.

In addition to ideas about Black people, ideas about White people and whiteness in the world were also essential to the experience of being transracially adopted. Several participants discussed or wrote about their views of and relation to whiteness during childhood. Cherise stated, "At a young age, Eurocentric features are what I craved. I have realized that the lighter you are, the more beautiful you are, the lighter your skin is going to mean you are going to be treated better, with more respect, dignity." Similarly, Austin stated, "I didn't ever want to be not Black. I just wanted to be White. Whiteness was the beauty standard. How I wanted straight hair. I just wanted straight hair so bad."

Another aspect of seeing Black and White for some was trying to fit into whiteness. Emilie shared about this during her interview:

> Being that I was raised by White parents in a predominantly White area, I spent most of my childhood from about fifth or sixth grade until college trying to assimilate into whitehood, like being White. If I decided that I didn't want to continue assimilating but wanted to continue trying to be accepted by my White peers, I felt like I would have no options as far as friends, as far as activities that I could participate in at my school.

The above experiences described by participants are explained further by McRoy and Zurcher (1983), who found that parental racial orientations and their associated behaviors were directly related to the perceptions of racial identity held by the children. Children with parents who had a Strong White Orientation associated less with Black people, held to common stereotypical beliefs about Black people, emphasized human identity over racial identity, had mostly White friends, and dated White people. In addition, they were given a higher social status by their White peers.

Another piece of seeing Black and White during childhood as a transracial adoptee was a feeling of discomfort specifically due to being with a White family. Alyson shared, "If my family went out to eat or I was with a parent at a store or entertainment place, if we interacted with a black person as waiter, cashier or worker it was hard to look them in the eye. I felt like a traitor of some sorts stuck between worlds, a word I now understand as shame."

Even as a child, Alyson noticed a powerful feeling in response to the racial dynamics of her transracial adoptive family and the racialized society in which she lived. Samuels (2009) conducted a qualitative study about the complexities related to race for transracial adoptees. One of the consistently present themes in this study was *managing societal perceptions of transracial adoption.* Alyson's experience illustrates this theme well.

COMMUNICATION AND SILENCE ABOUT RACE

When reflecting on what it was like growing up transracially adopted, participants shared about whether and how race was discussed with their families during childhood. Variation in both the amount and content of communication is evident in stories shared by participants. Some stories offer examples of communication that was memorable and meaningful, including explicit race lessons offered by some parents. Others illustrate a need for more communication and how the silence of the parents created a barrier to children wanting to bring up topics related to race.

Kaitlyn shared an explicit instruction she remembers from her mother:

> My mom lectured me and my brother about how we were to behave if we ever got pulled over, or if we were walking in a store and getting followed. When we found that [de-identified] was shot or the guy at Walmart, but my mom would always like explain to us why that happened. So, I think we just always sort of knew better, like how to react. Like, in stores, we never put our hands in our pockets or anything.

Similarly, Jacob explained the explicit lessons about race related to police and getting pulled over, saying, "My parents always harp on that. Like, always be respectful. Don't ever make any sudden motions. Always make eye contact with the police officer and be as cordial as possible."

Communication related to race is an aspect of racial socialization. The meaning and importance of racial socialization differs for White families compared to Black families. Black children are exposed regularly to racial lessons, whereas most White children are not (Daniel & Daniel, 1999). This difference is directly related to the racialized history of the United States. The meaning of being White (the dominant racial group) in the United States is quite distinct from the meaning of being Black (an oppressed racial group) in the United States. Therefore, racial socialization practices delivered by White parents to same-race children would look very different than racial socialization practices of Black parents with Black children. Because of differences in racial socialization (both from parents and from society), White parents raising Black children might be expected to use a variety of racial socialization approaches.

Racial Socialization for Black children growing up in a racialized society is seen as necessary to form resilience, gain healthy coping responses to racial adversity, hold positive in-group evaluations, and foster the development of racial identity (Bentley-Edwards, 2016; Hughes & Chen, 1997). In an extensive review of racial and ethnic socialization literature, Hughes et al. (2006) identified several categories of racial and ethnic socialization messages from parents, two of which are: preparation for bias and promotion of mistrust. *Preparation for bias* is the parental practice of raising their children's awareness of discrimination and racism. *Promotion of mistrust* includes practices that focus on the need for caution and distrust in interracial interactions. Mistrust can be transmitted explicitly through verbal warnings, cautions, shared stories of racism and discrimination, and explanations of systemic barriers to success. Mistrust can also be transmitted in same-race families implicitly as children observe their parents' interracial interactions or hear conversations among adults about people of other races.

The conversations about dealing with police or shopping in stores described by Kaitlyn and Jacob above are examples of preparation for bias as well as promotion of mistrust. These parents had some level of awareness that their Black children would need to know how to handle situations in which their safety could be threatened in such social situations. This level of awareness may be a more recent shift in the transracial adoption literature due to the growing visibility of police violence against Black people in the United States. Lee (2003) identified perspectives held and approaches used by White transracial adoptive parents (including both domestic and international adoptees). One of these was *racial inculcation*, the practice of actively preparing TRA children for dealing with discrimination and racism in everyday life. Explicit lessons communicated to adoptees regarding race sometimes illustrate this approach.

An explicit race lesson for Emilie had to do with the n-word. She remembered her father instructing her not to say it. She reflected on the conversation, stating, "I don't know how Black kids and Black families are talking about the n-word, but my dad was basically like, 'This is not a word that you use. If a White person says it, it's grounds for a fight.'" She also shared that she believes her family did their best to try to help if there was any issue related to race, but that there was a level of discomfort with the topic. She stated, "I think, for our family, it almost felt like the sex talk in that it's a little bit awkward."

Another aspect of transracial adoptive racial socialization mentioned in the literature is the idea that parents sometimes decrease their racial socialization efforts as their children grow up, presumably due to parents feeling uncomfortable or having reached the limit of their abilities (Lee, 2003). Barn (2012) calls this style of socialization in transracial adoptive parents *ambivalence*—characterized by parental confusion about how much focus should be placed on birth culture. Barn asserts that the approach to racial socialization enacted by White parents is directly related to their own understanding of race and racism.

There were also participants who did not receive the explicit race lessons they would have liked from parents. Cherise shared, "I wasn't getting taught about race. It wasn't a huge thing in the family. We didn't get talks about the police or anything like that. I kind of had to learn on my own and make those realizations and educate myself through the media or through social media." Alyson remembered, "The words, 'race, racism, White, Black,' were never spoken in my family growing up." Austin expressed, "They didn't teach me how to handle discrimination and anti-blackness. Like, it was never brought up."

In transracial adoptive homes, White parents, even without realizing it, function from the white racial frame, which socialized White people to think of White as "normal" and the "standard." White parents raising White children, as part of the dominant racial group in the racialized caste system in the United States (Wilkerson, 2020), have the option to ignore racial identity development in themselves and in their White children. Studies have shown that many White parents do not talk openly about race, or even recognize that they have a race (Bonilla-Silva, 2014). In racial socialization in White families, White parents are teaching children to navigate advantage rather than the disadvantage inherent in the racial minority family experience (Hagerman, 2017). This paradigm does not serve a Black child being raised in a White family and leaves out important aspects of socialization for Black children in the United States: *preparation for bias* and *promotion of mistrust* (Hughes et al. , 2006).

In the examples given by Alyson and Austin above, the racial socialization strategy used is termed cultural assimilation by Lee (2003). This strategy entails encouragement for the adoptee to orient toward White culture. This strategy was seen in a similar way in McRoy and Grape's (1999) qualitative transracial adoption study, in which one participant stated that there were never discussions about race in his home, even though he was one of three boys of color adopted by White parents. This socialization strategy ignores the white racial frame and the racialized caste system in which transracially adopted children are being raised. The prevalence of assimilation as a strategy is likely because cultural assimilation is the default strategy when no intentionally different effort is made by White parents. TRA children are immediately and constantly exposed to majority culture through their parents (Lee, 2003). As Smith et al. (2011) explain: As members of US society's dominant mainstream, White adoptive parents are positioned to transmit collective understandings, interpretations, knowledge and memories about whiteness, not blackness (p. 198).

DeBerry et al. (1996) describe Black racial socialization as a preparation for coping with oppression that begins as early as two years old. The racial socialization process teaches culturally relevant habits as well as values that will help children adapt in society and become competent in navigating life in a racialized society (DeBerry et al., 1996). This definition is expanded by Bentley-Edwards and Stevenson (2016) to include the transmission and acquisition of intellectual, affective, and behavioral skills with the goal of building racial *efficacy*. Racial efficacy allows for the reappraisal and negotiation of stressful racial/ethnic encounters. Such encounters occur within five psychosocial contexts: information and knowledge processing, relationship engagement, identity development, styles expression, and stereotype reproduction (Bentley-Edwards & Stevenson).

Another aspect of communication about race discussed in interviews and journal entries was whether participants could go to their parents about issues related to race. Maryama shared:

> I never talked about it because I felt like I couldn't get help from my parents because of the things that I was missing in my life. I think it's just because, in my head, I knew that they couldn't give me what I was asking for. But, now, I'm thinking back on it. If I did ask them, I feel like my parents would have tried to find a way to give me what I need or even just listen, because maybe that's all I wanted. I don't think I knew what I wanted.

Maryama's experience during childhood relates to a theme that has arisen in some studies that Black transracial adoptive children feel they need to handle situations related to racism alone. In Samuel's (2009) study of TRA multiracial young adults, several participants discussed not talking about issues of race and racism because they knew their White parents would not understand what they were going through.

One participant, Simone, stated that her parents were comfortable talking about the history of racial tension in the United States, and that she appreciated this. She said, "My parents were like, "We want you to know what happened. As a race, we're ashamed, of course." But they're like, "We don't want you to grow up not thinking that things were bad, because they were." This willingness on the part of Simone's parents to acknowledge the historical presence of racism and racial tension in the United States could be seen as an example of *cultural socialization* message described by Hughes et al. (2006), which includes parental practices that teach children about their racial or cultural heritage and history. However, an important aspect of this socialization by White parents is that it, by default, comes from a white racial frame. Therefore, the socialization that takes place continues a type of colonial control of the entire issue of transracial adoption (Willis, 1996); presenting the White parents as saviors with pure intentions, a characterization that commonly negates a necessary critique of the daily practices of racial socialization of Black children.

The level of competence of White adoptive parents in providing racial and cultural socialization for their children is a main concern in TRA (Vonk, 2001) research. In 1972, the National Association of Black Social Workers posited that White adoptive parents may not possess the necessary cultural knowledge and skills to parent non-White children. White adoptive parents have no personal experience with surviving racism on a daily basis (Berbery & O'Brien, 2011; Samuels, 2009; Vonk, 2001). White parents might not have awareness of the systems of racism that grant them, but not their Black children, unearned privilege (Vonk, 2001). Also, even with knowledge of racism and privilege, White parents might not be able to provide racial socialization in a way needed by Black children (Leslie et al., 2013). These experiences point to the strong need for trainings focused on racial identity development (group and individual), racial literacy, cultural humility, and anti-racist identity development for adoptive parents, which will be discussed further in Chapters nine and ten.

RACE MATTERED

Race mattered during childhood and teenage years, and the experiences participants shared illustrate how race mattered to their personal identity. Race mattered in that it was directly related to how the world saw them, how they saw themselves, and the stereotypes with which they were judged. During the transition to adulthood, prior experiences continued to shape their ideas of race. Race lessons given by parents were remembered. Adoptees shared about how prepared they felt for racialized life as a Black person. Some of the topics covered include personal style, friendships, managing image, experience of identity, and the assumptions of others.

Sadie discussed her personal style in relation to racial identity. She stated, "My style back then, I used to try to make it White, I guess. I was having such a hard time with my identity. I was trying to force myself to go in that direction just because the environment in high school."

Similarly, Emilie reflected on her time from 6th grade to college, and her choice to assimilate more with her White peers. She said, "I knowingly or unknowingly leaned into, and on, my White side as a way to assimilate and survive both school and life." In her interview, Cherise shared that all her friends were White during her growing up years. She said, "Honestly, I was okay with that. I didn't really think anything of it. It's all I knew and I didn't really want Black friends growing up." She then acknowledged, "I did get called Oreo: Black on the outside and White on the inside. At the time, it didn't really bother me. I kind of laughed it off because I think I did try to act White." Cherise went on retrospectively, sharing, "I was a token Black girl, I guess, now that I can see it. But now, it bothers me because I'm not White."

For some, the idea of identity and race, in retrospect, brought realizations of feelings of insecurity or lack of clarity related to Black identity. Cherise stated, "Looking back on it and my childhood I was a little Black girl who didn't realize that I could be beautiful and shine and still rock my dark skin."

Reflecting on how he understood race in relation to himself as a child and teenager, Austin talked about how he identified racially during childhood and teenage years:

> When I was younger, I used to identify as 'mixed' or 'biracial' and would use the 'part Native American' thing that so many people include. I realize that a lot of those identities were attempts to distance myself from my blackness. I wasn't secure in it, so I had to qualify it. And that was due in large part to my white family not accepting or even acknowledging my blackness. Despite the fact that I had all this proximity to whiteness, *other* people still saw me as Black and treated me as such.

One expression of how race matters is the management of the adoption story as it relates to race. Participants shared about the reactions of other people to the racial difference in their families, and the different ways they made sense of this as they were growing up. Alyson shared that for some time she did not tell her classmates that she was adopted, and that her father was White. She secretly hoped people would think her mother was married to a Black man, and she wouldn't have to explain her family to anyone. She then shared about what happened when people at school began to know her family and that her father was White:

> When people finally got wind of my White dad, they would ask me why I was adopted. And I didn't know what the feeling I felt back then was, but now I know that it was shame. The way they asked me made me feel like I wasn't normal or that I wasn't authentic in who I was. I used to lie about why I was adopted. I would just say that I was born in a bad neighborhood and that my mom wanted me to be safe but she couldn't afford to move (a subconscious story I told that I hoped would help people believe that I was indeed as Black as I looked because I knew saying 'bad neighborhood' would allude to the hood, and Black people live in the hood, right?). I literally had made this up as early as 2nd/3rd grade.

Alyson continued with her story, explaining the interesting racial image management that became a part of this experience for her:

> Contrastingly, around this same age, I was doing things to prove I wasn't like the other Black kids at school and that I was more like White people; (i.e.: not standing next in line to a Black person, ignoring or not playing with a Black person as to not be associated with them, try to overachieve to separate myself and be more like the White kids, talk about certain Black kids to make myself appear superior).

Alyson could feel that race mattered, both internally and externally, and clearly struggled with managing her racial identity in relation to societal ideas associated with race. Nuances of this theme, Race Mattered, are expanded through three subthemes: (a) Dealing with Monolithic Expectations of Blackness, (b) The Hair Journey, and (c) Experiencing Racism.

DEALING WITH MONOLITHIC EXPECTATIONS OF BLACKNESS

Participants explain the monolithic expectations of blackness that they faced. These expectations showed up as comments about not being "Black enough," feedback on mannerisms and ways of speaking, and lack of familiarity with Black cultural standards or pop culture during childhood and adolescence. Researchers focused on TRA have found that racial identity is an area in which differences are exhibited in adoptees (McRoy & Zurcher, 1983; Feigelman, 2000). Even in adoptive families that are not transracial, researchers have found that during adolescence, a preoccupation with one's adoptive status is common (Hayes, 2008). It would follow that in transracial adoptive families, the adoptive status is more obvious because of visible markers and questions from people about race and culture.

DeBerry et al. (1996) stress the importance of racial identity, particularly racial group orientation, for Black transracial adoptees due to the racial minority status of African Americans. Strong racial identity and group identification serve to aid Black people in coping with prejudice and discrimination, as well as prevent isolation and marginalization (Taylor & Thornton, 1996). Racial identity has been defined as the extent to which transracial adoptees use racial self-descriptors and are proud of or comfortable with their race (Lee, 2003). Grotevant (1997) considers cultural and racial difference to be a primary factor with which TRA adoptees must contend during the process of adoptive identity development.

Occurrences with friends was one way in which participants encountered monolithic expectations related to race. Participants described peers telling them they were White, or that they were not Black, or calling them names—all focused on race and identity. Austin remembered, "being called 'Oreo' and 'Black on the outside and White on the inside.' People telling me that like I'm not really Black or they don't see me as Black. Telling me I talk White." This same type of experience was described by Maryama and Cherise, both of whom were called "Oreo." Maryama recalled, "All I heard was 'you're not Black, you're White. Why do you talk like a White person? How does it feel to live with White people?' I HATED IT!"

In the following passage from a journal entry, Kaitlyn reflects on her experiences of comments made by friends, and how it caused her to believe things about herself:

> My friends who were White would always say things like, "you don't know what racism is because you have White parents," or they would say things like, "even I am blacker than you." I know now that none of what they say matters because they will never understand what it means to have dark skin and be

> stereotyped. But when you are just starting a chapter of your life and every little thing that a person says matters to you, that can mold your mind and make you believe things that aren't true.

Austin recalled a situation in his Spanish class during high school in which a Black student who had transferred to his school challenged him to a freestyle battle. He stated, "I literally said, 'I can't. I don't know how to do that. I'm so sorry.' And he said, 'What do you mean, you don't know how to freestyle?' I said, 'Oh, God. Look around. What about this environment makes you think that I would know how to freestyle?'" Austin described this as one of many moments when his blackness was questioned.

Another school arena in which monolithic expectations arose was school dances. In a journal entry, Alyson reflected on her feeling of not fitting into the monolithic expectations of blackness related to music and dances:

> People would know hip hop/rap dances and old school R&B songs that their parents had grown up on. I would not know any, 1) because I was too busy with after school activities to ever hang out or be immersed in my Black friends' or friends' family culture and 2) my parents were White and I was not exposed to a lot of music or vernacular or culture that my Black friends were. I feared school dances because everyone expected me to know these songs and dances. I did not. I also was very self-conscious about my dancing because it would be described as "dancing like a White girl." I think that is why in high school, I always drank before school dances. It made me feel more comfortable in my own skin. I also took hip hop, jazz, and ballet class in junior high so I could truly learn these types of moves. However, choreographed hip hop class never really helped me improvise on the school dance floor.

Alyson was joined by Emilie in this experience of attempting to know Black culture through dance classes. Emilie shared in her interview that her mother made the effort to take her to an African dance class. While she appreciated this effort in retrospect, she talked about feeling out of place in the class because of the lack of cultural context in her own life.

The above examples given by Austin, Alyson, and Emilie are relevant to Park and Green's (2000) point that evaluations of children's well-being define adjustment and maladjustment in individual terms, without considering the importance of the children's perception of their connection to the part of themselves mirrored in their racial or ethnic group, and their perception of how their racial group is perceived by society. In addition, related to the commonly assessed variable to self-esteem in transracial adoption, Taylor and Thornton (1996) explain that personal self-esteem and factors related to group identity, like racial identity, are not the same phenomenon. Personal self-esteem refers to how a person evaluates the overall self, unrelated to racial/ethnic group, whereas group identity is a bond with a racial group with common culture and origin. Because of this distinction, someone might report strong personal self-esteem, but may have weak ties to their racial group (Taylor & Thornton). Thus, in addition to self-esteem and the various measures of adjustment listed above, it is vital to consider racial identity and group membership in the case of transracial adoption. Hollingsworth (1997) conducted a meta-analysis on a longitudinal study on transracial adoption and concluded that transracial adoptees had lower combined racial identity and self-esteem scores than nonadoptees.

Participants described an ever-present awareness of being outside of what was expected in terms of blackness. Emilie shared that for her, there were things she simply never felt well-versed in:

> There are all types of things, from how to do your hair and what is a socially acceptable way to wear your hair, ways to care for your hair. Things like code switching-- I didn't so much understand code switching and which code you used, and how well you transitioned was important. Food. I didn't understand, how important it was to know how to cook certain foods or, how you seasoned certain things added to how people saw you. Or, different movies that people would reference.

Pop culture was mentioned by many participants as something that seemed to have monolithic expectations related to blackness. Maryama mentioned, "I found it hard to fit in with kids, especially during middle school. Kids at school would talk about movies and TV shows that all Black people watch. When they would ask me if I have seen it, I would respond with a 'no,' and I would get laughed at."

Many participants also mentioned comments about the way they talked and being told they "talked White." For example, Kaitlyn stated, "They told me things like, 'Oh, you talk like such a White person because you were raised by all White people.'" She went on to explain that most comments came from her White friends, who would commonly reference stereotypical understandings of blackness: "They would say something stereotypical like, 'You like fried chicken,' or something. They only know the stereotypical way. They don't really know like all the other stuff."

Because of the macrocosm of a racialized environment, participants were placed in situations where their ways of being based on their home environment and levels of cultural exposure, were questioned, labeled, criticized, and commented on. These experiences were a central part of how participants understood that race mattered and was central to identity personally and socially.

THE HAIR JOURNEY

The Hair Journey provides a description of a range of participant experiences related to how families dealt with caring for Black hair, the meaning of hair, and the journey of learning how to appreciate and care for their own hair. Hair was mentioned in interviews and/or written about in journal entries by most participants as an important aspect of identity that made race matter while growing up.

For some participants, there were memories of wishing for hair that was a different color or texture, and then gradually coming to appreciate their hair as it is. For example, Simone shared the following passage in a journal entry:

> Growing up, I always told my mom I wanted blonde hair, long blonde hair. I'm sure every girl has probably said that at one time. I did sports all throughout school. And it was always like, 'man, I want straight hair like slicked back.' I just thought it was low maintenance. And I found out that wasn't true. But that's how I always felt. So, I was just like, 'I want to be normal, I want my hair to be straight.' Because my hair is so kinky. And I just hated it growing up. But now I love it.

The same type of story was shared by Alyson, who shared, "I straightened my hair for the first time in eighth grade because my Black friends showed me how and they had straighteners. And that became a thing, straightening my hair. And I also felt prettier when my hair was straight. I don't ever straighten my hair, really, anymore [laughs] because I like to just embrace what I was given in life."

Another aspect of the hair journey for some participants was their parents not knowing how to care for their hair. Sadie shared:

> I think hair was something that I struggled with growing up because I never knew how to take care of it. When I was in the 5th grade, they cut it off. They cut my hair off when I was in the 5th grade so I looked like a boy. In high school, I would try my best on my own but I didn't really know until I got to college how to start taking care of my hair because I had like my friends showing me.

Emilie shared in a journal entry some of her journey related to hair, which also included her parents not knowing how to care for her hair and wanting to cut it off at one point. She explained that having Black hair and White parents was one of the things she struggled with most growing up. Emilie describes her struggle in the following passage:

> When I was young my parents used to put my hair in twists every day. In first grade the other Black girls at school started making fun of me for still wearing

> my hair that way, so they stopped doing twists. The problem was they didn't know how to do my hair any other way. Sometimes they would get my hair braided, but it was expensive and didn't last long with my hair texture so that was not a frequent occurrence. So, they weren't doing my hair and I didn't know what to do with it, so I wasn't really taking care of my hair. In third grade, my mom took me to a salon to get my head shaved because I wasn't caring for it and she didn't know what to do with it. The stylist suggested relaxing my hair instead, so we did. This ended up damaging my hair but I continued for several more years. Then in junior high I started straightening my hair every day to fit in. I stopped getting relaxers around 9th grade but resumed senior year of high school. I continued until I was about 20. By this point my hair was so damaged that I stopped getting relaxers.

There were also stories shared in which parents worked to learn how to care for participants' hair, or to find people to help. Cherise shared in a journal entry about her mom and hair and being proud of her mom for taking the time to learn to care for her hair. She stated, "It's not easy to do Black hair especially when your White and have no actually experience with it because your hair is nothing like it. I respect my mom for doing my hair, even though it usually ended and began in tears because she pulled too hard."

Interestingly, even with these efforts, Cherise continues to discuss the meaning of her hair, and how she didn't want it to call attention to her. She describes having an "irrational fear" that her White peers would know she had extensions, so she never wanted her hair styles to be too long or too short. She said, "I would spend that night stressing about the reaction of my teachers and peers. I had only felt real confidence when I had my hair straightened."

Maryama discussed her mom's efforts to connect with Black women at salons or in stores. She shared that her mom would ask Black women where they got their hair done, and if they could recommend a stylist for her daughter. During these experiences, Maryama noticed the reactions of Black women. She stated, "I did notice that the Black women would see my mom and be like, 'What are you doing?' I felt defensive for my mom. Like, chill, she's trying to help me." Kaitlyn recalled that her dad learned from hairdressers how to do her hair. "Hairdressers taught my parents how to take care of my hair. They taught them different protective styles to do. They really made an effort to know how to take care of me and my brother's hair."

Hair has a strong significance for participants as a tangible symbol of race, and something that set them apart from their families and White peers. Some participants reflected on this connection explicitly in interviews and journal entries. Jacob shared, "My hair was always an important part of who I was, but it wasn't until I began to learn how to care for it during my senior year. Learning about caring for my hair was something that took a lot of practice, and it helped me to find myself."

Expanding on this idea of the meaning of hair, Austin explicitly connected the lack of knowledge about hair care to race and identity in the following passage:

> I don't have memories of being told that it's wonderful that I'm Black, that its beautiful that I'm Black, and, this is how you take care of your hair, because it is different. And it's okay that it's different. Instead, I spent years having my fucking mother relax my hair and, because she's not a cosmetologist, she had no idea what she was doing. So, she would just paint my whole head with no-lye relaxer. Not the regrowth, just my whole head. I have chemical burns on the back of my neck because she had no idea what she was doing and it ate through my skin. My hair has been thinning for the last three years. I used to have these beautiful curls, they were so nice when I was 19 years old, and I'm so fucking mad that they're gone.

Each participant described a journey related to race and hair as a core aspect of the theme *Race Mattered*. Hair was present in the stories of participants as an unavoidable logistical issue that held strong symbolic significance related to racial identity and racial difference within family and school environments.

EXPERIENCING RACISM

This subtheme provides examples shared by participants of experiencing racism during childhood and teen years. These stories are shared to expand upon the description of how and why race mattered to participants as they were growing up and moving toward adulthood, and also how race and racism were factors which contributed to the shaping of their understanding of the world and themselves. Participants told stories of times they experienced stereotype threat, unfair treatment based on race, and explicit racism.

Kaitlyn reflected on how she realized that race affected the treatment received by her and her brother during middle school. She shared, "I started to realize me and my brother, who is also Black, would do the same exact thing as a person who was White. Yet the white person would get let off with a warning while we would have to spend our lunch in a detention."

Another school-related experience was shared by Alyson. This passage was part of a spoken word piece written by Alyson about her experiences related to race:

> I remember when we first learned about slavery
> 7th grade, world history
> Only Black kid in class and I was asked to read
> How I was less than human, and sold for mere pennies

That day at recess they played the masters, and I was their slave
Play along, I told myself, fit in and be brave

Racist comments from peers were another way that racism occurred in the school environment for participants. During his interview, Austin recalled:

> I remember the first time someone called me a nigger. I was 10 years old. It was in middle school. We were walking down the stairs to go to the buses. I knew that I was different and I knew there was anti-blackness, but it was the first time someone ever wielded it against me. It was like someone specifically said, 'You are Black and that's bad. This is the word that you use.' Everything before that was implied, or microaggressions.

Experiences of racism contributed to the understanding for participants that race mattered, it was a factor that meant something, even when that meaning wasn't clear. Emilie recalled, "Growing up, one of my best friends, anytime she would even so much as say the word Black, she would say 'no offense' as a preface to even the word Black."

A story from Maryama focused on a mission trip she took to Kentucky when she was 11 or 12 years old. She traveled with a group of seven friends, and groups from other churches from different states joined together, and Maryama was the only Black person there. She shared about this as her first experience of overt racism. She shared, "Every single day it was like, 'Oh so is it true that your people only eat, watermelon and grape drink and fried chicken?' It was just so blunt. They would make jokes, like, 'Your lips are so big.' I was just dumbfounded because they said that right to my face."

In addition to experiences with school and peers, participants also discussed experiences with family that showed them that race mattered, and how it influenced the perceptions of people around them. Sadie shared, "I remember my grandma telling me about how when I was little, my grandpa's friends used to always say something about them bringing me around. It used to make my grandma really mad. She told me about one time how this guy said, 'I see you're bringing the little [n-word] child around again.'" This story was one told to Sadie, and even though she doesn't remember the event happening, the story still stood out to her as part of her experience being transracially adopted.

Austin shared some things he remembered about racism in his family: "I remember my sister suggested naming our dog 'niglet' and when I said it, she told me I wasn't allowed to say that. And then there was the fact that my mom referred to rap as 'ooga booga music' and would mimic the women in videos." These memories were potent enough to remain a part of Austin's story into adulthood, and show the ways in which experiencing racism, even within his own family, was a part of realizing that race mattered, to him, and to others.

These experiences reflect the racialized caste system, described by Wilkerson (2020) as a foundational system that holds people in their position in the racial hierarchy and is built into the fiber of the United States. This caste system has been carefully and systematically sustained throughout history. Caste is similar to Feagin's conceptualization of the white racial frame; an old and continuing racial framing of US society. One way that caste and the white racial frame show up in participant stories is how it is an unspoken, sometimes unnamed foundation that seeps into the psyches of adoptees, making them aware of its presence without explicit education about what it is and how it informs daily life and the identities in a transracial adoptive experience.

Some participants discussed intuitively knowing that race mattered, but not being able to see it as racism at the time. Cherise shared, "Racism didn't really affect me growing up. But what it meant to be a Brown girl to me when I was younger was that my White peers were prettier than me, better than me, and more worthy. And that's what separated me from them." This example shows how the meaning behind race and knowing how it mattered was transmitted to this participant as a child even before she knew the word "racism." The racialized caste system and the white racial frame were already present in her life. Alyson reflects on this with the following statement from a journal entry: "I never knew what racism was as a child and certainly did not interpret my experiences during childhood as racism, although now it is clear to me that it was. I have words for what I observed, felt, and experienced: bias, institutional racism, personally-mediated racism, vicarious racism, and internalized racism."

Because caste and the white racial frame are implicit and insidious, retrospective reflection becomes a common way for its presence to become visible. During childhood and adolescence, a feeling was present that was yet to be named, yet clearly held weight in the lives of adoptees.

Chapter 3

Between Two Worlds

This chapter moves forward in the lives of participants out of childhood and adolescent experiences into emerging adulthood experiences related to transracial adoption and being between two racial worlds. Emerging adulthood has been described as a critical developmental period that forms a bridge between adolescence and adulthood (Hope, Hoggard, & Thomas, 2015). Emerging adulthood commonly refers to ages 18–25, and sometimes ages 18–28. During this period, emerging adults engage in extensive identity exploration, and experience the feeling of being in between two life phases -- childhood and adulthood (Hope, Hoggard, & Thomas, 2015; Munsey, 2006).

Black emerging adults who were adopted and raised by White parents comprise the sample for the study described in this book. The reason for focusing on the emerging adult age group is that emerging adulthood is the time during which Black transracial adoptees will potentially leave the family home and experience life in the world without an association to their parents' whiteness as an influence in real-time or potential buffer in situations related to race. Also, because emerging adulthood is a time during which identity exploration is highlighted, it seems plausible that a Black emerging adult who was raised by White adoptive parents might enter new social environments in which race becomes salient in new ways. This experience might spur a new process of racial identity exploration, especially if the White parents had not discussed race, or fostered a colorblind approach to parenting their Black children.

The distinction of emerging adulthood in the transracial adoptive experience also aligns with previous transracial adoption research. In a qualitative study by McRoy and Grape (1999), exploring the significance of skin color in transracial adoption, ten Black transracially adopted adults were interviewed (ages 21–32). Most participants in this study described not beginning to accept their Black identity until entering college (emerging adulthood). For many participants in this book, college was the first time they were exposed to racially diverse spaces. In McRoy and Grape's study, one participant shared that it was not until adulthood that he began to make Black friends and started to feel more comfortable with his Black identity. These research participants' accounts are also reflected in recent nonacademic stories of transracial adoptees told in the media. For example, Chad Goller-Sojourner, a transracial family coach and performer who was transracially adopted by White parents in 1972, shares that it was not until college that he could make his "descent into blackness and out of whiteness." Goller-Sojourner added Sojourner to his name in his early twenties, a time during which he says he finally fell in love with himself and with being Black (NPR, January 26, 2014).

Emerging adulthood is a time during which participants leave the protection of the proximity to whiteness with their white families, and venture into the world in a new way bringing both challenges and opportunities relating to racial identity development. Another aspect to this experience is that due to proximity to whiteness, transracial adoptees living with white families will experience a particular position in the caste system based on race in the United States (Wilkerson, 2020), and that position undoubtedly shifts when a Black emerging adult leaves the home of their White parents.

According to Wilkerson (2020):

> A caste system is an artificial construction, a fixed and embedded ranking of human value that sets the presumed supremacy of one group against the presumed inferiority of other groups on the basis of ancestry and often immutable traits, traits that would be neutral in the abstract but are ascribed life-and-death meaning in a hierarchy favoring the dominant caste, whose forebears designed it. A caste system uses rigid, often arbitrary boundaries to keep the ranks apart, distinct from one another and in their assigned places.

The *assigned place* of a Black child or adolescent in a White home is a different *assigned place* than a Black emerging adult independently navigating the dynamics of our nation's caste system. The caste system is rooted in power as well as who is seen as worthy of resources, who receives respect and authority status, and who is assumed to be competent (Wilkerson, 2020). In this chapter, adoptees describe the experience of being in between two racial and cultural "worlds" of Black and White (two distinct caste positions). Between Two Worlds explores how transracially adopted emerging adults are experiencing and understanding race as they become adults.

Most transracial adoptees shared that there were times they felt either too White or not Black enough in Black spaces or that they would be told they talked White, acted White, or were White. Participants also described feeling discomfort related to this feeling of being in between two racial worlds, and the social experiences that reinforced that discomfort. Emilie shared, "I think that because my complexion is lighter, people often say I act White, because I was raised by White people and I don't have a lot of experience with Black culture because I wasn't raised with Black culture." Simone shared that the issue of being between two worlds shows up in certain conversations with her boyfriend: "Sometimes he makes comments like, 'Wow, that was a really White thing of you to say.' I'm like, 'What do you mean? That's just how I was raised.' A similar reflection came from Sadie in a journal entry:

> Even to this day, it genuinely bothers me to be called 'White.' Today I still hear that certain things I do are because I was raised by White people. Just because I was raised different than typical Black people from Detroit, it started to make me feel a little out of place with the Black community. I am always too White for Black people, and I am too Black physically for White people.

Alyson continues with this idea of being "Black enough" with this passage from a journal entry that shows the crux of feeling in between two racial worlds: "Why I still feel I have to prove that I am Black enough. . . . I don't know. It is clear to others, but not to my inner child. It is an oxymoron and hypocritical, because I often find myself shaming myself or hiding or stifling my true self as to not appear as Black in White spaces, yet I do the exact opposite around Black people to try to prove I AM Black enough."

The effect of being between two worlds was described by Maryama as insecurity with the following statement from her interview: "I get very insecure about myself before even meeting people, because I fear that rejection, and I know I shouldn't. But, based on past experiences and how I have been rejected by other people just because of my background, that's why I've become more of a homebody." This feeling of insecurity was echoed by Cherise as she reflected, "I just feel like I need to be surrounded by more Black people. But sometimes, I do feel held back. I feel self-conscious because I feel like I might be judged by my Black peers, and they'll think, 'Oh, she's not down. She's not Black enough.'" Sadie explains this as a feeling of pressure, stating, "Now I feel like there is this constant pressure like I have to live up to what a Black person acts like and lives their life, which I don't."

When discussing his experiences related to race, Jacob shared, "I'm more comfortable around people I have more shared experiences with. But taking it out of context that would imply that I'm racist towards Black people. But I don't think that's the case." He went on to explain that the comfort of shared experiences is related to race and ethnicity for him: "Racially I feel African American. Ethnically I would say I'm more along the lines of Caucasian. I identify with some of the struggles, but I come from an upper-middle-class family. I'm a very privileged child. In that way, I haven't experienced the same struggles as a lot of my racial peers."

Another way that being between two worlds was present for some participants was with being categorized by other people, which links to the racialized caste system described by Wilkerson (2020). Austin stated:

> The thing that I've always thought was interesting was White people's obsession with figuring out 'what I am' and trying to make me not Black. Black people, and everyone really, has that same curiosity when they see people and they say, "You don't look like you're just Black." Black people's curiosity is usually, "What are you mixed with?" They are saying, "I see your blackness, but there's something else there." Whereas, for White people, it's, "What are you?" Because I talk the way that I talk and I am the way that I am, but I have this skin color. But it's not the same skin color that they're used to. And I'm also very gay and very out as gay. It doesn't make sense to them. And so, there's this obsession with figuring out what I am and why I am the way that I am.

Wilkerson (2020) explains that beneath each racial label connected to physical features is centuries of history and assigning of assumptions and values to physical features. She refers to these connected features and assumptions as a "historic flash card" that automatically calls up expectations about a person (p. 18). Austin's physical features and behavior didn't clearly match expectations dictated by the caste system, and he noticed people attempting to categorize him racially.

Each participant shared the feeling of being between two racial worlds. In the following three sections, subthemes (a) They Don't Get It, (b) Feeling the Divide in Friendships and Dating, and (c) Feeling Disconnected from Black Culture are described to expand the description of this shared transracial adoptive experience.

THEY DON'T GET IT

Adoptees share experiences of being misunderstood by family, peers, and others in relation to racial identity. Being between two worlds is described by participants to include the feeling that other people do not understand the unique experience of being Black and having been raised by White people, and the frustration that sometimes accompanies the experience.

Sadie spoke about this during her interview when she shared, "I feel like I experience some sort of racism from both White and Black people. It gets on my nerves when people say that I try to 'act Black.' I AM Black. I act the way I act, and my race shouldn't determine how I am supposed to act."

Interactions with families are another source of transracial adoptees feeling misunderstood. An experience of her father "not getting it" was recalled by Cherise during her interview:

> We would never just have a normal conversation. There were times when we were yelling at each other. I remember him saying, "I should have just taken you to a Black college because you hate White people," and all this other stuff. Just because I started to be more comfortable in my identity as a Black woman, he didn't like that and just kind of dismissed that for me being prejudiced towards White people. And I said, "But most of my friends are White. I've been surrounded by White people and it hasn't been a problem, but I'm just starting to realize my role and how important it is. And me loving myself and being comfortable in my own skin shouldn't be such a huge problem to you." And I was telling him, "If I had Black parents, I wouldn't be having a lot of these issues and a lot of these problems." So, it was just frustrating.

Another arena in which participants experienced others who didn't get it is at work with peers. Emilie wrote about an experience she had with a coworker in which she felt misunderstood and offended. She stated:

> DB and I had a hard time working together for other reasons, but I believe one of them was that I didn't fit his idea of what either a White girl or a Black girl should be. I cut my hair and went natural about a month into the school year, so I wore my hair in a fro, or other natural styles, for about 6–7 months. By around February or March my hair was finally long enough to flat iron. I did so and wore it down to school. He approached me and said, "I see what you've been trying to go for, but I think this (my straight hair) is more you." I was so mad because first, my hair is no one else's business but mine. But more importantly, him saying straighter, whiter hair was more me felt like an attack on my blackness that I had worked so hard to love and be proud of.

Another description of a work situation that resulted in the feeling of "they don't get it" was shared in a journal entry by Alyson. She explains her role as an advanced medical student, and how her unique history and background brings with it a specific skill set, but that it often leaves her feeling perpetually drained and misunderstood:

> In the academic setting, I work on a weekly basis to explain bias and racism in healthcare and society to tenured professors, medical students, and experienced physicians. I am used as a liaison between worlds because it is a skill set I have acquired by being raised by White people but knowing firsthand what it's like to operate in a White society as a Black person. My Black friends tell me I am their spokesperson because the White people relate better to me and are more willing to listen and not interpret my passion as anger or threatening. My White

> friends tell me I am brave for bringing up these very important matters because they don't have the vocabulary or examples to explain these realities, experiences, and history themselves. No matter how hard I try and how hard I prepare and how well I articulate over and over again to translate how racism works to the people in my PWI [predominantly White Institution], I always feel left drained and unaccomplished. I am exhausted from this and too often I end up just internalizing in silence because I'm too tired to constantly feel the burden of being the self-nominated and publicly-expected one to explain all the time.

Maryama experienced her family "not getting it" when she attempted to explain her choice to join a sorority, and why her sorority is exclusive to African American women. She shared the following in her interview:

> I just joined this sorority last semester, and it's from, a NPHD sorority, so it's part of the Divine Nine and it's all African-Americans. I told them about that, but it goes way over their heads. I was trying to explain to them how excited I was—you know, to find some sisters, and they were just like, "Okay." I just want them to understand, like, the basis of it. I told my family, and they just don't get it at all. I have an older sister. She was like, "Well, why can't I join?" And, I'm like, "Oh, my gosh! Let me just have this thing to myself." And, she's saying it jokingly, but she's genuinely like, "Well, why can't I do it?" I say, "Okay. Let me explain this to you. It's the history. We were founded in 1922. There was segregation and all this stuff happening in Indiana. That was the melting pot of the KKK, and these women formed this group so that they could get an education for other Black women. And so, it's continued that way." So, then, my sisters and my family see it as, "Well, that's not being diverse." I'm like, "Oh, my gosh. That's not the point." But, it's always an argument about race with my family.

As a Black woman, Maryama was excited to be a part of one of the Divine Nine sororities, and the meaning was rich. Her frustration came in when that meaning was not understood and was dismissed by White family members. In this moment there was no shared historical context that could be drawn upon to aid in mutual understanding.

Kaitlyn shared an experience in which she felt her unique situation as a transracial adoptee was not being understood by her friends who were also adopted. She stated:

> I don't really think they get where I'm coming from in terms of race because they've never had to experience it the way I have. My whole family's White, but all my other friends - they're White and their families are all White—they're all the same. I love my family, but like it can be kind of awkward sometimes, like when I'm trying to tell my friends things. So, I think they just don't get what I am going through, so we just don't talk about that stuff much.

Austin describes an interaction with an acquaintance in which the racism Austin experienced from his family was invalidated. He stated, "We were talking about our families. I mentioned how racist my family was and the guy interjected that he 'doesn't think my family is racist.' To which I replied 'which one of us do you think knows better?' He instantly got quiet." Austin continues, explaining how this interaction reminded him about how easily people assume that White people with Black family members can't participate in racism. He shared:

> I know that his follow up would have been 'they adopted you, how can they be racist?' The idea that a White person or White people can't be racist simply because they have loved ones that are Black, whether they be friends or family, is truly reprehensible. It all sort of adds credence to the idea that there is only 'one type' of racism, and that's the scary overt kind. But the more insidious version, the one where Black people are constantly invalidated and victimized is the one that comes from White people that are supposed to be people that care for us.

The above stories shared by participants provide examples of how people "not getting it" is directly related, for these participants, to being transracially adopted. There is the idea that people don't grasp the process of fighting to claim a racial identity different from the racial identity of family, don't understand that having pride in that identity and engaging in exclusive activities or groups that nurture it is important, and don't see how being transracially adopted and experiencing racial difference within one's family is an experience all its own. This dynamic is reflected in past transracial adoption research. In a dissertation study conducted by Bumpus (2015) Black adoptees, ages 25–72, had higher levels of racial identity when adopted by two African American parents as opposed to two White parents. While most of these participants were older than participants in the current study, Bumpus considers relevant factors. For example, transracial adoptees reported that their parents de-emphasized contact with upper and middle-class Black figures, making it more likely for transracial adoptees to accept a more stereotyped perception of Black identity. In addition, White TRA parents most often raise their Black children in mostly White environments (Barn, 2012). Because of this, Black TRAs are less likely to experience natural connections with the Black community and could miss out on learning the value of interconnectedness with the Black community in building resilience (Bumpus, 2015).

FEELING THE DIVIDE IN FRIENDSHIPS AND DATING

Participants describe their experiences with a racial divide among friend groups or in dating experiences. Caste can again be seen here with "assigned places" based on race that makes having friend groups or partners of different racial castes complicated. Interactions with friends and dating relationships were arenas of life that intensified the feeling of being in between two racial worlds.

Some participants shared about noticing or anticipating the reactions of other people in terms of race. Simone described, "I feel like sometimes when I've dated White men, I've just—like I almost try and not be Black, if that makes sense. Or I try and tone it down. But I think that's just because I'm more scared maybe about what people will say." This idea of being "too Black" for White men and dating came up for Emilie as well. She told a story in her interview about a time when she was dating a White man, and she first cut her hair and started wearing it natural. She stated, "As soon as I cut my hair, I sent him a picture of it. He was like, 'Oh, okay.' And then we hung out again, and it was very weird. At the time, I didn't really see it, but I think it was that I looked too Black for him."

While he expressed some uncertainty about coming to any conclusions, Jacob shared that he wondered about whether his race, and associated stereotypes about Black people may have affected dating for him in high school. He discussed the fact that he attended an all-White private school, and he shared, "I think race might have been the cause for me not dating anyone in high school or middle school. But I'm not entirely sure if certain expectations or certain stereotypes played into why I didn't really have a dating life or not."

Another aspect of experiencing a racial divide in dating and attraction was described by Sadie. Her experience was related to her own interests changing rather than anticipating the reactions of other people. She wrote in a journal entry, "Before I even came to college, I only liked White guys. I used to not even be attracted to Black guys. Then I came here and I was just around Black people all the time and I just kind of felt my taste in guys just shift completely." Sadie continued, explaining how part of the attraction had to do with shared understandings. "It is a race thing but it's also just kind of more than race. Because if I were to be with a Black guy there would be a lot more understandings that would already just be known." Sadie's experience points to the importance of results from McRoy and Zurcher's 1983 study about racial identity and transracial adoption. Their results showed that parental racial orientations (white or multiracial) influenced adoptees' perceptions of racial identity, beliefs about Black people, and comfort with Black people. As Sadie's exposure to Black culture increased when she entered the college environment, her racial orientation shifted, changing her views of herself and others.

A racial divide in friendships was very memorable for Alyson and Maryama. They shared their experiences of having two entirely separate friend groups based on race. Alyson's experience took place during college:

> I had two distinct different friend groups in college. The ones that I lived with and spent most of my time with were White. Whenever I wanted to spend time with my Black friends, or go to a Black Student Union event, it became a thing. I just remember feeling very nervous to tell them, "I'm going to hang out with so-and-so," and they knew that I was going to hang out with the Black people tonight. They didn't want to have any part of it, and they got annoyed. I remember their faces, their nonverbal cues, and their reactions to that. Even when I invited them, they did not want to be a part of that, and it felt like they felt I was betraying them.

Maryama also described having two distinct friend groups divided by race. She shared, "I wouldn't get invited to parties or people would be like, 'You can come, but don't invite your White friends.'" She continued with describing what it was like to tell her White friends she was going to a party with mostly Black friends in attendance: "They would ask, 'Well, why can't we come?' And, I'm just like, 'You guys would be the only White people.' And then, that would stray them away, and they're like, 'Oh, okay.'"

Maryama explained that she liked each of the two environments and wanted to experience both. She said, "I wanted to go to both, but then, I would get criticized, 'Oh, Maryama was at that White party, drinking beer and, you know, sitting around listening to music.' I guess that wasn't like what the Black kids would do. I didn't see any wrong to either of them."

Participants' experiences of a racial divide in dating and friendships were a central component of the feeling in between two worlds. Friendships and dating relationships were arenas in which the racial divide rooted in the racialization of the society in which participants live was especially potent and meaningful.

FEELING DISCONNECTED FROM BLACK CULTURE

Transracial adoptees in young adulthood frequently feel disconnected from Black culture, and they must handle comments and judgements from others about their racial identity. Participants expressed how being disconnected from various Black cultural markers increased their feeling of being between two worlds, and sometimes not knowing where they fit due to their unique combination of adoptive and racial identities.

A reflective story shared by Jacob about attending a fall welcome event for Black students at his university offers a glimpse into his experience of disconnection and being between two worlds. He explained that he finds it hard to relate to people of color because of a lack of shared culture. He states:

> I know that racially I am Black, but I'm starting to understand the primary differences between ethnicity and race, it's a matter of culture, language, and other vital experiences that bind the two together to make a person who they are, ethnically. For instance, during my first week on University of Cincinnati's campus, the African American Cultural Resource Center had a barbecue and it invited all African American students to attend. I wanted to go and so I did, but during my time there I felt out of place, like I wasn't supposed to be there. Obviously, that's not true, but for whatever reason I felt that way. I felt alone and isolated in this crowd of people that were just like me even though I'm typically an outwardly extroverted person. I felt like we hadn't shared the experiences that would help me to develop those connections that I so desperately wanted to develop with my fellow African American peers.

Jacob's description shows the extra cognitive effort and discomfort that comes along with being in Black spaces, something that for people raised in Black spaces, would potentially bring increased feelings of belonging and comfort.

Maryama echoes the feeling described by Jacob, wanting to know more about Black culture and make connections, yet feeling out of touch:

> It still is hard for me in college because I still strive to "fit in" with my African American peers. People "joke" around and tease me but that really hurts my feelings because they don't understand how much I desire to actually know what I don't know about my "culture"; the culture of struggling, and being below the poverty line and going to family reunions with chicken and soul food while listening to hip hop and R&B. I never got to experience that unless I was with a friend. Sometimes I wonder what my life would be like if I was ever adopted by a Black family. Would I be more accepted?

Most participants shared that there were aspects of Black culture from which they felt disconnected and described the situations in which those aspects would come up. Sadie discussed not knowing certain things that most of her Black friends grow up knowing. She stated, "I didn't know about sew-ins when I came to college. I would ask questions, they would say something, and I'd be like, 'I don't know what that is.' They'd be like, 'That's because you're White.' I'm like, 'I'm not White.'" She went on to explain her feelings in response to such situations: "It makes me feel like singled out, awkward or kind of dumb for not knowing. It depends on the situation, but it makes me feel like I'm not being respected enough for what my actual race is." This feeling was echoed by Cherise, who described constantly feeling, "as though I am not Black enough, and have to prove myself every day. But I am Black, and you don't have to 'act Black' to *be* Black. Those stereotypes and microaggressions can be really damaging and alienating."

Emilie described an experience common in her life related to feeling disconnected from Black culture:

> Just today I was at lunch with three Black coworkers and they were asking me if I've seen School Daze, which I now know is a Spike Lee movie, then proceeded to list off ~20 classic Black movies they would have thought I'd have seen. Although I like these coworkers and they would never make me feel less than or not Black enough for not having seen these movies, I still did and that is a hard feeling to swallow.

For Austin, there were times the feeling of disconnection from Black culture arose in specific social arenas. He shared:

> I was still very nervous to go into typically masculine Black spaces like barber shops. I would make my husband, then boyfriend, go with me, and he had to set up the appointment. I'd never had my hair cut by a Black person before. And I didn't know any of the language. I would say, "What do I want him to do, you know?" And so, he had to teach me the language and I still struggle with the language sometimes.

The following passage from Alyson shows how this feeling of disconnection relates to the experience of being between two worlds. She stated, "In my White family, of course I am the most knowledgeable of Black pop culture, and they often look to me for answers as if to speak for the entire Black community. But with my Black friends, I am probably considered the "least cultured."

Some participants shared that part of the experience of feeling disconnected from Black culture, and people noticing, was having to explain. Emilie stated:

> It can be awkward because you don't want to admit that you don't know something. So, it depends on how close I am to the people who have made this reference that I don't understand. If it's people who I'm close with, I'll often ask, or, if it's not, I'll kind of just fumble my way through and pretend I understand. Or, sometimes, like more recently, I've become a lot more comfortable with kind of making a joke out of it, "I have no idea what you're talking about. I was raised by White people." And most people understand then.

Maryama described sometimes wishing that Black friends would teach her instead of confront her about not knowing certain things, because being reminded of things she hasn't learned brings up feelings of embarrassment and longing. She explained:

> Somebody will be like, "Well, who is this person?" I'm like, "I don't know. I've never heard of them in my life." And, they're just like, "Are you serious?" I'm like, "Well, teach me," you know? You don't know what you don't know, and I can't blame my parents for that. Even today, people assume that about me in college who don't know anything about my background, and I say, "No. I still don't identify with what you're saying." So, it gets annoying after a while. I don't want to always have to explain myself. I say, "I was raised by White people."

Most participants explained ways in which they felt disconnected from Black culture, and how this added to the experience of feeling in between two racial worlds. Race, ethnicity, and culture is salient for Black transracially adopted emerging adults because until emergence into independent adulthood, experiences related to race have been connected to the family identity, which includes whiteness. Participants described an increased exposure to racial diversity during college. Their race was highlighted by peers, and with greater awareness of one's race comes the exploration of the significance and meaning of race (Hurd et al., 2013). If raised in a mostly White environment, the experience of associating regularly with peers of color may introduce a new internal conflict that could come with the suggestion of Black peers that one is not *really* Black, or not Black *enough* (Samuels, 2009), as was echoed in participant stories here. Transracial adoptees find themselves between two racialized caste positions, struggling to know the rules, ways of behaving, and expectations for both, but never feeling completely a part of either one.

Chapter 4

Growth in Black Identity

In this chapter, transracial adoptees share stories from emerging adulthood when their Black identity became more prominent, embodied, and understood. Participants describe processes of change during that transformed their perspectives and gave their blackness new meaning. Growth in Black identity was a central aspect of adoptee narratives, and seemed to accelerate specifically during emerging adulthood due to exposure to new environments, people, organizations, and media sources.

Some participants described becoming more aware of certain social issues related to blackness. For Cherise, growth in Black identity began when she became more aware of issues of police brutality and began exploring more race-related topics through social media. In her interview, she shared about the process of coming to understand that being in a White family didn't mean that she had no place in the Black community, and that it did not exempt her from being vulnerable to the experiences faced by Black people in the United States. She said, "The color of your skin can mean whether you're going to die at the hands of people who are supposed to be protecting and serving you. My eyes were suddenly opened." Cherise described her mindset shifting as Black issues and topics were becoming more important to her. She said, "My blackness was a gift, that was another thing that I had slowly began to learn. That definitely changed my core self."

Simone discussed in her interview that she connects her awareness of racism with comfort with her Black identity: "I notice, at least now, over these last five years, as I've gotten more comfortable with, I guess, my blackness, racism is still alive. And it's still a big issue." This awareness, for Simone, came during emerging adulthood as the racial diversity in her life increased.

Learning some Black history and watching certain Black-centered television shows was relevant for Jacob during the summer before starting college. He discussed watching the Netflix show, *Dear White People*. He said, "I think I was trying to make myself more aware of African American culture and that kind of stuff. I watched a lot of documentaries and ingested a lot of information about, I guess, my race in America."

For Alyson, her larger process of self-exploration included the solidification of her Black identity and an interest in Black history and culture. She stated:

> I think five years ago is when I started solidifying my identity in my own way. I was able to kind of delve more into understanding who I was. I journaled a lot. I started meditating, started training for a half marathon and running in silence and thinking without outside noise. And then also, I had traveled to Ghana twice right before that. I think I was just alone in my thoughts and was able to be, like, "Who am I?" And with that, I feel like I came into my own identity. And then, things that mattered in the world started mattering more to me. And so, I began my journey of really understanding Black history and culture. And once I started understanding things more, that's when I started bringing these topics up to my parents.

Sadie unexpectedly delved into the Black community when she came to her university. Because most of her friends in high school had been White, she said she assumed she would continue that trend, and find mostly White friends in college. She was surprised when the following event occurred:

> It all kind of changed when a friend of mine in my scholarship group brought me to a frat party. When he said frat party, I was definitely not thinking of a Black frat party. I didn't even know Black frats existed. That was really the night everything changed for me. I can easily admit that at the party I was very confused and kind of shook at the things that were happening. The way people were dancing, the types of songs that were being played, the way people were dressed. I felt awkward and out of place, but something about the atmosphere is what I liked. I remember walking back to my dorm that night, I was really happy and excited. I started to associate myself more with the Black community on campus, which is not what I was expecting. I had never been around this amount of Black people in my life before, and it was definitely apparent how they had their own culture. There are certain unspoken understandings, but I enjoyed being around them. For the first time in my life, I found myself only attracted to Black guys. I didn't look twice at White guys anymore. I started to feel myself being more comfortable with my Black side, and for the first time, I started to feel like I was beginning to find my identity. From there on out I just identified myself as Black.

While the Black frat party was new and unfamiliar, there was something about it that Sadie appreciated and was drawn to. It ended up supporting a spring forward in her Black identity development. Being steeped in an environment in which her blackness was reflected back at her in a group setting encouraged a new growth in her Black identity.

The stories shared by adoptees related to growth in Black identity illustrate how interaction with the world outside the nuclear adoptive family was the catalyst for an increased embracing of blackness for participants. These stories also reinforce the importance of exploring group identity development for transracial adoptees as a salient factor in racial identity development. For Black emerging adults raised by Black parents, the nuclear family would have been the source of information and experiences to help with the embracing of blackness throughout formative years. For transracial adoptees, the nuclear family can be the factor limiting exposure to Black communities and culture, increasing the importance of opportunities like going to college in the lives of adoptees.

For some adoptees, part of embracing blackness was the gradual realization that they were doubting themselves or feeling negatively about themselves. They start to identify their irrational thoughts as internalized racism. Alyson shared that she began to see how systems had influenced her perspective on race and on herself. She wrote in a journal entry:

> The system of bias and institutional racism cultivated the way I see Black folk. I was subconsciously trained to have racist ideals and I was Black myself!! I internalized this as well and also didn't have pride in my own Black skin. It affected my confidence. And to this day I still don't believe I am as naturally smart as the "smart and fast reading/comprehending" White men and women in my medical school. I have achieved some of the highest achievements one can in academics. I am part of the 1 percent who have made it all the way to become a physician. Yet, I still have imposter syndrome.

While this realization was unpleasant, Alyson found it important because it caused her to connect her own identity with the identities of other Black people surviving the same systemic issues related to race. Austin also shared about how growing into his Black identity meant facing the negative feelings he had about himself, which he connected to having been raised in a mostly White environment. He stated, "It's been a big journey for me to understand my blackness and how the life that I was raised in caused me to devalue myself as a Black person. Having been deeply submerged in whiteness with my family and the environment I was raised in, I truly didn't love myself."

As evidenced by these stories, growth in Black identity for transracial adoptees in emerging adulthood can include realizing and grappling with internalized racism. Emilie shared in her interview that growth in her Black identity caused her to have a new rift between her and White people in her life. She reflected that this was a time in her life when her friend group moved from being majority White to being majority people of color. She stated, "At that point I felt like the crack between myself and all the White people I knew widening even further because, now that I was educating myself, I was like, 'Wow. Things used to be terrible, but things are still pretty crappy.'" Emilie continued to describe this transition in her identity, and the discomfort and struggle that came along with the things she was learning about race and the White people to whom she was close. She said:

> That was really hard for me, especially being that my parents are White. Everyone that I grew up with that I was still friends with was White. My early college friends were White. Like, there were so many people that I cared about who are White, but it was hard to, sort of, separate my feelings for White people in general and the terrible things that had happened in the past and were still happening today from those people. So, I ended up pushing a lot of those people away, whether they deserved it or not, and some of them did deserve to be pushed away out of my life. But that was probably one of the hardest transitions I've ever made. That's sort of how I moved into adult life was—my transition with how I saw myself and how I interacted with the world due to race wouldn't really have started until around then. Now I've gotten to a much healthier place where the people I love are the people I love, and I love them for a reason.

Emilie described another piece of this transition when she felt that she had to prove that she wasn't White, and engaged in behavior that she regrets in retrospect. She became involved in a racial awareness organization on her college campus, and became close to a group of friends who were all people of color. She shared, "When I look back on the way we treated my roommates and my other group of White friends, it was wrong. We were unkind. We would talk about them behind their backs, mostly based on the fact that they were White." In recollecting these experiences, Emilie shared her understanding of why those things happened:

> I think it happened because I felt like I needed to prove myself almost. I had been, basically acting like, and almost wishing, that I was just White for all these years, and then, I finally was okay with the fact that I was not White. I was proud of the fact that I was Biracial and Black and White. I felt like I needed to prove to other people that I was proud of this. And, I obviously took it way too far, which I think had a lot to do with the group of people that I had become friends with and, like, the way they interacted on their own, but it was because I felt this need to, like, prove that I was Black enough and prove that I was not White.

Each participant expressed times in their lives during which they came to understand their Black identities in new ways, whether through learning new information, having new interactions, noticing new feelings and thoughts, or engaging with new communities.

EMBRACING BLACKNESS

These anecdotes describe times during emerging adulthood when participants began to embrace their blackness as an important and defining aspect of self. For some, this was related to new interactions that helped them feel their Black identity more thoroughly, for others this had to do with accepting and loving their physical characteristics associated with being Black, and for some participants it came in a new perspective or a new claiming of the identifier of "Black." Embracing blackness was shared by most participants as central to growth in their Black identities.

Austin described, during his interview, a casual interaction with his husband's grandmother that helped him sink deeper into his Black identity. He shared:

> One of the first times that I felt a Black person see my blackness in a very different way was my husband's grandmother. I was making coffee and, for the very first time—I had never heard anyone do this—I asked her, "How do you take your coffee?" And she said, "A little bit darker than you." And I thought, "Okay. I get that." You know, and no one had ever talked to me like that before, just like a Black person to a Black person in the way that she expected I would understand. And I did because, you know, it was easy, but, that's a very distinct memory for me. I felt I was being welcomed into a community because we were using common language and a common understanding.

For Austin, this casual, everyday type of interaction was incredibly significant in his process of feeling part of the Black community. This type of interaction is the kind of thing that would have happened on a daily basis in Austin's life had he been raised in a Black family, but for him, it stood out as an initiation into blackness.

For Simone and Maryama, part of embracing blackness was acceptance of their physical characteristics as Black women. Simone recalled:

> When I was growing up, I was made fun of because I was dark, too, because I wasn't Biracial or anything. But it's nice now because like social media loves it so much. Which, I mean, it's kind of sad that it took it so long to get to that point where people accept women of color. But now you see people, all the actresses, I love looking at their Instagram because it's like—the top comments are like other Black women saying, "Oh, you're so beautiful." That's what I like to see.

Maryama remembered starting to love her hair and skin when she got to college. She discussed joining an organization for Black women on campus, and that the group stressed the importance of loving one's hair and skin. She said, "That's why I went natural. I cut my hair freshman year of college, and I've loved it ever since."

Kaitlyn joined an all-Black sorority to strengthen her racial identity. She said, "Since it's all Black—I never really grew up with that, so I thought that it would just be nice to see what that would be like."

University provided Sadie with the opportunity to be immersed in a community of Black peers. When asked how the change of environment influenced her, she stated, "I think my opinions about race have changed a lot. In high school, I didn't really identify as Black because I was just so used to being around White culture. I feel like I'm a lot more open-minded about it now. I used to really not embrace my Black side but now I do, so that's a big change."

Emerging adulthood brought a similar process of embracing blackness for Cherise. She described a process of taking pride in being Black and in being a part of the Black racial group:

> It has taken me a long time to be comfortable with my blackness but it's a mindset that I have to have every day. And then when I did start to realize, "Okay, I should love myself. Black people have so much to offer, and they are amazing." And there's a lot of great stuff that they can do and continue to do, and they invented certain types of music, and do so many things. It took me awhile to realize, though, we are awesome.

The process of embracing blackness brings pride and knowledge but it can also include realizations about experiencing oppression, and finding empowerment in group identity. Alyson shared her experience of realizing that she had been trying to please others by going along with external expectations, and how letting that go was a part of embracing her blackness and finding empowerment. She stated:

> I have acquiesced to their domineering culture, yet am resented for being the very person they wanted me to be. I could have been myself all along and they would have still hated me. Was it worth the mask all these years to change myself to assimilate and be accepted but hated regardless? Naw. I'm tired. Been time to start living as the person I've always been inside. I am consciously trying to be more unapologetic for my blackness. When I see Black leaders being unapologetic in their ranks in congress or physician leaders or athletes, etc., I am more empowered to do the same in my community when I speak up or speak out.

INTERSECTIONS

The growth of Black identity intersects with other salient identities for several participants. Sexual orientation, religion/spirituality, age of parents, and gender identity intersect with Black identity. Growth in Black Identity occurred simultaneously and in connection to these other relevant identities, and would have developed differently without those aspects of self.

For three out of nine participants, a journey related to sexual orientation intersected their racial identity development. Maryama shared, "Since I've become more comfortable with my sexuality, I can be more comfortable with my race and my background. I have come a long way since my freshman year in college when it comes to self-identity and me being confident in who I am."

Austin expressed a similar idea, stating:

> For me, a lot of my identity and like the development of my racial identity was coupled with being gay. Being Black, and being feminine, and, and not being masculine meant that I wasn't often accepted into most Black spaces, especially by Black men. The homophobia within hypermasculine Black spaces, like that will always be there. But my husband goes through that too. But my husband also knows how to code switch a little bit better because he was raised by Black people.

Austin continued to explain the intersection of sexual orientation, gender and race and how during emerging adulthood at university, things began to come together more for him in terms of a community that reflected his own identities:

> When I was in high school and growing up because of the way I expressed my gender and my sexual orientation, even if I wanted to find other close Black friends, we didn't fit into each other's lives, solely because I didn't necessarily subscribe to the same beliefs, especially around gender and gender expectations. I didn't like sports. I did theater, all that stuff. Then I went to college and I met queer Black people and it was more closely aligned with what I was experiencing and what I was looking for because these people also shared this other identity. Being young and Black and queer, that queerness is what really, a lot of times, kept my other young Black counterparts from me. Then I went to college, and when I started finding other Black friends, they were all queer and Black, or they were all Black and allies, and comfortable with people who are not straight or who were gender variant.

Cherise, in her interview, discussed the intersecting ways she experiences her identities in relation to society. She shared, "The way that society does view Black women and men is in a stereotypical, too loud, or like they have an attitude, and a lot of times women are super disrespected. I'm a woman, I'm Black, and I'm gay. That's a lot stacked up against me sometimes, so that's hard." She also discussed another layer of intersection, which was salient for her and other participants: religion. Cherise told her story of sexual orientation, and how she experienced rejection from her dad that was rooted in his Christian religious beliefs. She remembered her dad saying, "All right. You can either be gay and live that lifestyle or follow the Lord and marry a man but suppress your gay urges." She continued, sharing how this rejection caused a feeling of deep-rooted shame that she understood to be internalized homophobia. She said, "I think a lot of kids deal with because it's hard, especially when you do grow up in a Christian home or a really religious home. And when you're not accepted by your parents, it just kind of destroys you, and it sucks because they're supposed to have your back."

Cherise also shared her own struggle, as someone who identifies as Christian herself, trying to reconcile oppression happening in the world with the ideals she was trying to live as a Christian. She stated:

> As Christians, you need to have that mindset, be open-minded and love everybody. But I couldn't, because I was so full of anger to the injustices that were happening. And I'm like, "If that makes me a bad Christian, I don't know what to tell you." Because a lot of stuff, continually is happening to Black people and that's really hard to cope with and be loving towards.

When Maryama discussed religion, she expressed that she experienced a divide due to her sexuality and also her style preferences in terms of worship. She talked about attending a nondenominational church on campus that includes some of the Black Christian tradition, and how this felt better to her than the style of church where she was raised. As she experienced growth in her racial and sexual identities, she noticed that her values differed from that of her parents. She shared that her views and values, especially related to sexuality, differ from her parents, and that it continues to be a divide between them. She stated:

> Religion, my parents were very conservative, and we went to church every Sunday. My mom is so concerned about me losing my faith, and that's not true. I definitely believe in God, and I definitely, like, will go to church. I just don't like the old school sitting in pews, you know. I want to go out and be able to praise, and not necessarily force my religion down people's throats, but be able to, you know, praise with other people in a different way.

Some adoptees spoke about seeing racism firsthand within their churches, and the struggle that caused them with their church and with religion in general. Simone stated:

> Being a Christian is not an easy thing, especially while Black. It's even worse on weeks where hot button issues are preached about. Like police brutality. My pastor preached on that one week, and it became very clear who was a closet racist. One man literally stood up and said "if you look like a criminal, you deserve to be killed." I then promptly stood up, turned to him and said, "Jesus was crucified, and I think we all know he wasn't White like you all want to believe, so where does that leave us?" The older White gentleman then stood there stuttering and trying to justify what he had said. The point I'm trying to make is that, of all the places, there is so much racism and prejudice in the church. You really have to stay grounded to your faith to get you through these encounters.

Cherise also talked about a time when race was discussed in the mostly White church she grew up attending. She gave an example of how congregation members controlled the narrative supported by the church:

> It was uncomfortable, honestly. Because they would talk about how there's still a lot of racism in the world. And my pastor, at the time, he'd be like, "We, as a church, we don't talk about these things, and there is a lot of racism within the church," and we would talk a little bit about police brutality. I did enjoy some of the stuff he would talk about because he would be on the side of like how Black people are treated poorly, and there's a lot of injustices. I guess afterwards, he made an apology because there was a police officer in one of the services and he felt kind of attacked by that sermon. Yeah, there really hasn't been too much talk whenever I'm in church about those certain things.

Parental age also influenced the tone of the home. Sadie was raised solely by her grandparents, who are White. She shared, "The whole identity thing was kind of hard for a while. A lot of the standards that I grew up with were typical White household standards, especially with my grandparents being a whole generation older. It was way different than everyone else my age is raised."

Several participants shared experiences related to growth in Black identity that were inextricable from other salient identities. Those intersections included sexual orientation, gender, religion, and age of parents, and they added complex layers to the process of development in addition to race.

INFLUENCES, PATHWAYS, AND SUPPORT

Participants describe people, organizations, experiences, media, and social media that were helpful in the journey of developing Black identity and learning about Black culture and history as a Black person raised by White parents. During emerging adulthood, individuals explore many aspects of identity: (a) work/career, (b) school, (c) love/relationships, (d) worldview, and (e) race, ethnicity, and culture (Munsey, 2006; Reynolds, 2016). Reynolds et al. (2016) found that parental ethnic and racial socialization facilitates psychosocial adjustment and ethnic/racial identity for Black emerging adults. These researchers also found that ethnic/racial socialization was associated with greater ethnic racial exploration in Black emerging adults, as well as a stronger sense of affirmation and belonging to one's racial/ethnic group. In addition, Reynolds et al. found that a positive, nurturing, and connected parent-child relationship affects ethnic/racial identity development. Considering Black emerging adults raised by Black parents, this all seems understandable. Yet, when considering Black emerging adults raised by White parents, the question arises of whether closeness and nurturing from White parents would facilitate racial or cultural identity development. Same-race parents provide a model of blackness, whereas White parents must be intentional about exposure to culture, and so increased racial identity development is likely less a default result of a connected and nurturing relationship between Black children and White parents. That is not to say that it is not possible, if the White parents are in fact intentional, aware, and knowledgeable about the importance of race and culture for their children, and active in their pursuit of a continued understanding and supportive presence for their children's identity exploration.

For adoptees in the current study, Growth in Black Identity was strongly influenced by sources of support beyond the nuclear family. For Kaitlyn, a refreshing influence was a teacher in middle school. She describes this teacher's intentional focus on race in the following passage:

> She was one of the only Black teachers I ever had. And in February, when it's Black History Month, none of our teachers really talked about that, but she was our English teacher, and she had us do a museum project where we had partners and we researched different aspects of Black culture and did a big museum thing. Like, my parents didn't really teach me a lot about Black culture, but she took the time to teach everyone about it because she felt like it was important for us to be educated on Black culture, because most of the time, we're really only educated on White culture in the United States. A lot of the White students didn't really like the project because they thought that there was no reason to do

> it, but I think for the Black students, it had a different impact because we never really get to learn about the Black culture in schools. It's always White culture.

Other pathways and influences came through community involvement, which sometimes happened in the form of organizations. Sadie discussed in her interview that being at college and just having proximity to Black people and getting involved in community was helpful in growing her Black identity. She shared, "Coming here, just being introduced to these many Black people I just kind of started involving myself in the Black community. I think I started becoming a lot happier especially with my identity after that." Another influence for Sadie was her involvement in her Black Greek organization. Prior to going to college, she didn't know that these organizations existed, but they came to be an important part of her racial identity journey. She shared the following about the influence of joining a Black sorority:

> I'm in the process of joining a Black sorority. For some people, this is their whole life. It's very tradition-based, like culture-based, and I think that's what I like about it. It's a very good networking opportunity. Like since I started joining, I've met a lot of different people from other schools that happen to be Black too. It's a very connecting type of thing to do. I never would have expected myself to do it. I'm happy with my decision though. The more I was around events and stuff like that, and the more I saw how their bond was, I was like 'that's something I want to be part of.'

Maryama also had support in growing her Black identity. She said, "I have my girlfriend, my sorority sisters, and that's all I need. If I ever need anything or if I'm feeling questionable about my identity, I'll have a discussion with them."

In addition to Black Greek life, there are programs on college campuses focused on race, racial history, and race-based support. Both Maryama and Emilie talked about the influence of these programs on their racial identity development. Emilie shared, "I went to a program at [college] for minorities in political science after my third year of college, and that, for me, was really the time when I spent the most time with people who looked like me and people with origins that were similar to mine." A combination of popular culture and campus events helped Jacob with his growth in Black identity. He shared:

> 'Dear White People' was really good about explaining African American culture and college life. I would say that it helped me to understand a little bit more about my situation, and also helped me to understand how I can better identify with my own race as well. I am trying to be more emerged in the community that I try to identify more with. I have attempted to do so a variety of ways, I suppose. I went to a panel about being Black at [college] this past Wednesday. I

networked there. And I extended my hand out a lot more than I had previously at the prior event.

Social media was another pathway to growth in Black identity mentioned by several participants. Simone shared the affirming influence of social media, stating, “Social media promotes it so well. I’m really into Twitter I think every first or second of the month, a lot of people I follow do the Celebrate Women of Color, which is nice because I see people on there who are like 10 times darker than me.”

Cherise shared her experience of social media providing much-needed Black representation. She shared, “Thank goodness there’s so much positive Black representation. ‘Black Panther’ is the perfect example because here you have a movie that has a mostly Black cast. I am seeing these strong Black women fight bad guys and I am seeing these Black men not portrayed has thugs and criminals. And I think that is so amazing and empowering.”

Personal connections, friendships, and spending time in the homes of Black friends is another way that some participants felt they were influenced and supported in growth in Black identity. Alyson and Maryama talked about friendships they had that gave them the opportunity to be included in the experience of a Black family. Alyson shared:

> In high school I still had my best White friends from grade school in the neighborhood, but most of my friends and my best friend was Black. I think that’s when things changed for me. We became very close. And through being included in her Black family I got context. They were like my family, and different from my family. Different in some of the values, conversations, interactions, but same as in families love, provide, exist, operate as unique and wholesome units. Some key differences included going to Black church and how religion was expressed, expressions of affection, strict rules, what movies we watched and music we listened to, how one’s value as a person was communicated, and the depth of conversations about God, boys, love, reality, safety. Spending time with this family affirmed to me that Black families weren’t some aberration that was poor, unfit, unintelligent, poor mannered, reckless household. It’s not what I thought that it was based on what I saw downtown or the very limited understanding of what I may have seen on TV or in movies. I connected with her family so much. Her mom was like my second mom.

Similarly, Maryama discussed spending time with families of close friends who are Black. She said, “I’m able to be in their families and listen to stories from uncles, grandparents, and I can hear from their side of the story, because I’ve only heard from my White family and their side. So, it was really eye-opening. Now, I do feel more connected or interconnected with them.”

Additionally, close connections with strong, positive mentors were mentioned as a pathway toward growth in Black identity. Austin shared in his interview about supervisor he had after graduating from college. He stated:

> This woman very much so ended up being this incredible mother figure that I never had, that was very pro-Black. She taught me all about activism, and feminism, and community organizing, and radical politics. She changed my entire life. Changed my life. Saved my life, honestly. Like, I get emotional talking about her. She's, she's the mom that I needed. She was the one teaching me language to be able to respond to anti-blackness. Like she's the one that taught me the, the word microaggression. She taught me about systems of power. She taught me about, disenfranchisement, and marginalization, and how that stuff worked. And I was able to take that and practice it with my husband because he understood that language. There was like this paired belonging with progressive movement forward into the like specifics.

Another important influence for some participants was connecting to racial history of the birth family. Alyson experienced a self-mentorship that began with solo travels to two different African countries. She explained in a journal entry the monumental value of these trips:

> During my junior year of college, I traveled alone to Ghana to find myself. The next year I went back. Two years later, I went to South Africa. During these trips I do believe that I "found Myself." These trips contributed to the shaping of my identity as a biological daughter of an African Immigrant, descendant of slaves, and who I am as a Black woman in America. These trips gave me spiritual awareness, context, and purpose. It was like I stepped off the plane onto the red soil of my ancestors, and was instantly enlightened. That sounds pretty dramatic, but it truly was the culmination of these trips that in a stepwise fashion, I gained the identity and voice that had always been within me, but myself and the world was so blind to for all the years of my life. These trips helped me invite light and love into my life thereafter and it gave me the insight to choose my friends and companions wisely and offered the wisdom of how to pursue my purpose on this earth.

A variety of influences, pathways, and supports were discussed by each participant as they told their stories of experiences related to race as transracial adoptees. Participants articulated the importance of those influences, and how they were especially nurturing when raised by White adoptive families. Black Greek organizations, friends, mentors, co-workers, social medial, and travel provided a much-needed social context fostering group identity development.

Chapter 5

Views of Family Related to Race

A primary and complex task for transracial adoptees is coming to terms with oneself within the context of the family and culture into which one is adopted, while navigating the development of a racial identity that differs from the adoptive family. This chapter includes a range of thoughts and reflections on family related to race, providing a vignette of the various and sometimes conflicting feelings about family that can be present for young Black adults who have been raised by White parents, and how the experience of being Black creates a unique perspective on family values, ideas, and behaviors. The theme Views of Family Related to Race will be described first. Following will be descriptions of two related subthemes: (a) Having to Teach Family, and (b) Allegiance, Loyalty, and Gratitude.

In her interview, Sadie described her parents' opinions related to race, and how her relationship to their views shifted over time. She stated, "They're just really set in their ways. They have their opinions about it and they don't really change. That's why I think it took so long for me to be able to form my own opinions on race. I started feeling in different type of way about them, disagreeing maybe." It is clear from Sadie's statement that the process of becoming an adult caused her own identity process to alter how she was relating to the opinions of her parents regarding race. She became more independent in her thinking as her experiences expanded to include interacting with more people of color at university.

For Emilie, views of family included seeing efforts made by her parents and also acknowledging that, in retrospect, it was sometimes not enough:

> I think the most difficult part was realizing how much I do feel I missed out on and how, despite my parents' best efforts, there are a lot of experiences and knowledge that my parents just could not provide for me. It's hard not to be resentful of that, but I know my parents did the best they could to provide us with the best life they were able.

Emilie's statement is consistent with some previous qualitative research on transracial adoption. For example, in a qualitative study conducted by Samuels (2009), a participant discussed how, as an adult, she realized how much she missed, and that she felt some anger, even though it was combined with gratitude for the unique perspective on race she gained from her family.

For Kaitlyn, there were difficult family dynamics around race, but she also felt that her family was supportive and understanding about issues of race. She stated:

> One thing that has bothered me now that I'm older is how my dad will sometimes say that he is a Black parent because he has raised Black kids. I think what he means to say is that he understands more of what Black people go through in terms of racism, but he will never truly understand the struggles that Black people as a race face. Even though he will say that from time to time I still love him very much and my mom too. I am blessed to live with a very strong and supportive family and one that is diverse in many ways. Me and my brother can understand the things that we go through in terms of racism and my parents are always there to help us with our problems and the differences that we face in the world.

Kaitlyn's analysis of her father's meaning when he states that he is a Black parent shows how her perspective as a transracial adoptee allows her to see two racial worlds. Willis (1996) writes that the socialization that takes place in White transracially adoptive families continues a type of colonial control of the entire issue of transracial adoption, presenting White parents as saviors with pure intentions. This characterization commonly negates a necessary critique of the daily practices of racial socialization of Black children. The white racial frame is the default for a White person, psychologically speaking, so that Kaitlyn's father *grants himself* permission to label himself as a Black parent, without considering the inaccuracy of his statement, which is entirely obvious to his daughter. But because she is his daughter, and loves him, she puts in the effort to analyze and understand his statement, while still holding true to her own interpretation of his words as a young Black woman.

Cherise discussed a common struggle she had attempting to talk to her dad about race, and discussed the support from another family member. Her home was a source of both frustration and connection. She said:

> A lot of times my dad would make me feel dumb during arguments about race. Sometimes I had this idea of what I wanted to say to him and then actually voicing those opinions and thoughts wouldn't come out right. And then he would get the wrong idea or just not understand. So, sometimes, my stepmom would be like, "Oh, she probably means this." That was always super nice. There's definitely a connection, and we definitely bonded over that. That was really

awesome because it's nice to have somebody who has your back in those things especially when it's really important to you.

Having a multicultural family of siblings that were all adopted brought a unique view of family related to race for Simone because she wasn't alone in being racially different from her parents and siblings. She reflected, "In my family, we have a lot of different cultures. My adopted family is very Dutch. My oldest brother is Caucasian and Puerto Rican. I have a Biracial brother, and I have another brother who's mostly Polish. And we're all adopted. Growing up we always like welcomed everybody's cultures." This sharing is an example of the potential variations present in transracial adoptee narratives.

Reflecting on their current relationships with parents, several participants described feeling a sense of distance from family members when topics of race came up with family members. Jacob stated, "I love my dad. And I love his personality and all. But like, it can be really hard to interact with him sometimes because of that. Because of his views and all that. And it can be awkward."

This feeling of distance was described in other ways, as well. While Alyson's parents were open to hearing her talk about race, in her interview, she expressed a longing for a deeper level of engagement and more mutual understanding on the topic. She shared:

> I wish that I could talk to my parents fully authentically about all things that I have experienced and how I feel and for them to truly understand. I think that as a child you always want to connect with your parents in various different types of ways. And I feel like this is one of them where there is a disconnect. And maybe from naivete on their part or just never really trying to understand, like reading about it. And, like, If I prompt them to read an article about race, they'll read it. But I don't know the context in which they're reading it and then our discussions are just mostly me talking.

Alyson also reflected on how her parents were lifelong learners and how she felt their selectivity in terms of what they educated themselves about avoided topics relevant to race and her experience of race. She said, "They read all the time. My dad reads magazines about money, business, politics. I'm, like, "Could you have read about Black history and taught me about that? Could you have taught me about things about Africa or anything like that?" Alyson's reflections show, again, how the work of interpreting her parents' behavior related to learning about race and discussing racial topics is solely on Alyson to bring to the forefront. She is left wondering why this topic does not appear important to her parents, when it is something that affects her daily and is something they will only learn with intentional efforts.

Similarly, Austin noted that being educated on topics of whiteness and race was not a priority for his family members. He stated, "No one in my family has done any type of work to understand their privilege to like understand what it means for them to be a White family and have a Black child." Austin shared a story of a call he made to his mother to discuss issues of race and racism in the family. He said that the first things his mother said in the conversation was, "We raised you to be a White boy from the suburbs." He continued, discussing how this lack of awareness displayed by his family, as well as racism he witnessed from them, has affected him. He said:

> About a week ago, in therapy, I really sort of lost my mind about my relationship with my family, specifically my mom. I have internalized the damage done from witnessing my family express racist views. My intention is that I will be writing her a letter detailing the many things that I am struggling with compartmentalizing. I can no longer pretend like hearing my family express racist views has not had a lasting impact on me.

The statement made by Austin's mother is an extreme example of *cultural assimilation,* one approach to racial socialization in transracial adoptive families identified by Lee (2003), in which the adoptee is encouraged to orient toward White culture. Historically, assimilation has been most prevalent in transracial adoption. In addition, however, Austin had the additional complication of digesting racist views expressed by his family. This experience shows clearly the presence of the racialized caste system, described by Wilkerson (2020) as the ever-present social structure in the United States, in the home in which Austin grew up. It is unique to transracial adoptees to have people who share their race attacked by White family members. Austin's statement about the difficulty he has had with compartmentalization illustrates the amount of effort needed to thrive after this experience. Now that he is an adult and not dependent upon his family for survival, he plans to share the truth of those events from his perspective as a Black man.

HAVING TO TEACH FAMILY

Participants commonly shared stories of having to teach their White families about race, racism, and racial history. This aspect of the theme Views of Family Related to Race shows a piece of the transracially adoptive family dynamic that participants have to continually decide how to approach, even in emerging adulthood.

Cherise described being with her extended family, and finding herself trying to teach them about cultural appropriation. She stated:

> I was with my grandparents and I have aunts and uncles there and we had a huge conversation about cultural appropriation, and we talked about hair and what I thought White people were appropriating from Black culture and it was just, it was kind of a mess. But nobody really saw eye-to-eye. My cousin was literally just like, "yeah I just feel like she's just trying to say that there are a lot of people, a lot of women, a lot of kids, a lot children and men, Black men, a lot of people who are all the time being told that certain hairstyles aren't okay and how, when a White person wears it, it is celebrated or is trendy." So yeah, that was a huge conversation I had with my family and it just kind of ended in a mess.

A similar story was shared by Maryama. She stated, "My sister and I were talking about dreadlocks and why it's unacceptable for her to do that. But, she's like, 'But, it's acceptable for the Black girls to get White girl hair.' And, she's talking about weave, and I'm just, like, I don't know how to answer that." Maryama didn't feel ready to be the expert, and yet she felt frustrated that her sister continued to question her view. She said:

> I don't know the history of it or the background of it. I just know that if she were to show up with a weave or dreadlocks or cornrows, it would be offensive. But, I kind of explained that to her, and she was getting mad. And, it made me feel uncomfortable because she wants these answers from me like I know. I'm like, "I'm learning too, you know. You have to understand that." But I don't think they understand the struggle that I've been going through. They ask questions about things they're genuinely confused about, but they already have their own preconceived ideas, and then it's kind of hard to change their mind because they just come back with a rebuttal.

Austin also shared a time when he responded to his sister's statements in order to teach her about "colorblindness." He said, "I was like, 'You can't say that you don't see color. That's such an invalidating thing to say and also wrong, because you do.' And so, I was talking to her and she's coming around to it more."

As Jacob learned more about Black history during the summer after high school graduation, he began to learn things that caused him to challenge his dad's understanding of certain topics related to race. He recalled an exchange with his father after watching a documentary about the Black Panthers:

> I think what my dad said was that they were a pseudoterrorist group. I was quick to correct him and say that that was not the actions of the Black Panthers but the actions of like, one of the syndicates that spun out of the Nation of Islam. My dad was like, "I was alive during that time. You don't know what you're talking about." But it was like, he's talking about the 1980s. So, the Black Panther

> Movement had like, really died by then. It was replaced by other more extremist like, African American groups . . . like the Nation of Islam.

Jacob thought quietly for a moment, and then said, "I think . . . Like with anything that has to do with politics, my parents and I often disagree." This example shows the way that the racialized caste system is present in transracial adoptive homes, even if unconsciously. While Jacob's father may feel that his lived experience of being alive in the 1980s was more valid than the information Jacob learned in the documentary, he had no knowledge base to understand that his experience of being alive during that time was limited to the perspective of a White, privileged male, and that the information shared in the documentary was from an entirely different social lens. If Jacob's father had been able to understand this, he might have realized that he was not an expert in issues of race and that shifting to learn from his son would be an important way to show respect for his son's racial identity. Similarly, in Maryama's story, her sister's repeated challenge of Maryama's perspective placed Maryama on the defensive. Instead of her sister learning from her, she left Maryama feeling disheartened and unheard.

Some participants described a sense of resignation, realizing that certain family members were not open to learning new ideas about race. Kaitlyn shared, "I think my dad's mom doesn't understand a lot of the stuff that comes with being Black in a White family, but I don't really try to explain it to her, because she's just set in her ways. It doesn't really do any good to try to talk to her about it."

Being in a position of teaching family about race—or not being able to do so - was described as part of being a transracially adopted emerging adult in today's world. Alyson uses an analogy to attempt to explain this unique situation:

> Having to teach my family about the complexities of race and history and culture is like trying to teach a fiscally irresponsible adolescent, who hasn't learned adding and subtracting yet, financial literacy in order to run a business. Access to the learning environment with a teacher and textbooks and encouragement, but no context, no skills, no capacity for understanding, no willingness to invest in that learning, distracted, no background knowledge, no incentive toward meaningful action.

She continued, expressing a feeling of futility related to the conversations she has with her parents in an attempt to teach them about race and relate her personal experiences related to race. She stated:

> In present day I feel like I overtalk about race to my parents. Every time I'm home, I start some type of dialogue about race, usually with my mom, then I

end up talking her to death for like 3 hours and I'm starting to feel like I am bombarding them with things they don't want to talk about and that they may feel that I'm that girl who always obsesses about race topics. They understand the diversity work I do in my school but I don't think they realize how race is something I've dealt with, still deal with and think about on a DAILY basis and how much a part of my life it is.

Because some family members have not prioritized learning about racial topics, the weight of convincing family members of the importance of race is left to adoptees, and this can feel like an overwhelming and frustrating task at times. The following section explores the next, equally complex subtheme, Allegiance, Loyalty, and Gratitude.

ALLEGIANCE, LOYALTY, AND GRATITUDE

Using a lens of allegiance and loyalty to the family, participants reflected on complex situations with family members. Also, participant stories describing gratitude about parents' efforts to support them in specific ways related to race are included here. Transracial adoption family dynamics are unique in that there are sometimes coexisting, yet seemingly incompatible components of relationships present. Some participants describe an awareness of discomfort, lack of support or feelings of frustration due to racial identity, but this does not cancel out the feelings of love, connection, and gratitude present in those same relationships.

One way that allegiance and loyalty to family showed itself in participant stories was the tendency for some participants to not confide in parents about things related to race in order to protect them. Simone said, "I tell my parents some stuff. Some stuff I keep from my parents because I know they get upset. There has been some stuff I just don't want to tell them because it does nothing but hurt them. If I'm okay with it, then that's all that really matters."

Similarly, Emilie shared that her parents probably don't know that she feels like she missed something in terms of exposure to diversity and Black culture. She shared, "I don't 100 percent know that I would ever tell them because they have done so much and I love my parents deeply and I know that hearing that would hurt them, especially because they always did their best." This awareness of parents doing the best they could was mentioned by several participants, and usually accompanied a sense of gratitude and loyalty. Maryama discussed her parents' efforts to expose her to African American culture in an academic way through trips to museums and similar educational pursuits. She said she didn't start to appreciate this until she got to high school. She shared:

> I saw that my parents were actually trying to make me more knowledgeable about my culture. I always make sure I thank my parents for that because I'm like, "You guys didn't have to do that. You could have just raised me as, you know, just normal and not teach me about my background and just had me learn it in school." I'm very thankful for that and I feel like they tried their best.

Maryama also addressed in her interview how bonded she feels to her parents, regardless of their differences. She said, "I feel like my bond is so strong with my parents right now. Just because I have differences with them and my beliefs, I'm not going to not feel that bond anymore. I still go to them." Even though Cherise experienced struggle with her father, she found solace in the level of interest and awareness shown by her step mom. She expressed her gratitude, stating, "My step mom is super socially aware and always had my back in the heated arguments that I had with dad. I will always deeply appreciate her for that."

Jacob has gratitude for transracial adoption in general. He expressed that he felt it was a good option to help expand opportunities in some ways. He shared about what he thought transracial adoption provided for him in his statement, "I think it [transracial adoption] allowed me to focus more on schooling and who I am. It gave me an opportunity to stay away from some of the more disruptive cultural elements of the African American community like gangs and that sort of thing." In Jacob's sharing, there is an acceptance of a monolithic perspective on blackness that includes stereotypical understandings of the Black experience in the United States. Jacob's words are a poignant example of the unconscious handing down of understandings rooted in the racialized caste system. This kind of perspective is in alignment with the common view of White adoptive parents as "saving" their adoptive children from a stereotypically informed imagined life of poverty and chaos based mostly on race and racialized caste. Such imagined illustrations of lives lived by Black people are an example of what writer, Chimamanda Ngozi Adichie (2016) named, "The Danger of a Single Story." In such stereotypically held characterizations of people, the richness of variation, within-group experiences, subcultures, meaning, and much more, are lost. Without personal experiences and more exposure to Black community, the single story about Black people will be the default due to the racialized caste system at work in the structure of the United States.

An insight shared by Alyson had to do with realizing what her parents didn't give, but also what they did give. It felt important for her to acknowledge the following:

> My parents didn't talk about race and racism or tell me that I belonged even though my skin was different or tell me that I am loved even if people treat me

> different because of my skin . . . but what they did do is treat me like I mattered, they always made me feel like I belonged in their family through their equitable treatment of me and my sister, they stood proud when they introduced their family to strangers, they had pictures of us at their work, they supported me in anything I ever wanted to do or tried to do. I think this was their way of telling me that my skin did not make any difference whatsoever in their level of love for me.

Continuing with the idea that family was a mixture of disappointment and fulfillment, Austin acknowledged that while needs related to race were left unmet, there were other components of his family's influence that were supportive. He stated, "It was a lot easier for me to unlearn sexism and be supportive of women than it was for me to unlearn racism and be supportive of Black folks because I was raised by my mom. All negative things aside, she's an incredibly powerful woman. My feminism was encouraged."

Some participants shared stories that included some confusion about where White family members stood on issues of race and racism. An example is a story reflected upon by Simone. Her brother had friends who used the n-word, and she addressed this with him. This inspired the following thoughts:

> I know my brother obviously doesn't think that. He doesn't share the same point of views. He has a Black sister. So, I know he doesn't think that. But like hanging out with his friends sometimes I feel like so awkward, because I want to speak up and say something. But—there's only been a couple times where I've like heard it. And they've never directed it at me, which I guess it's—I mean, it's bad either way. But it's like, what do you really do in that situation, because that's your brother's friends? So, it's like, does he secretly think that? Like sometimes I get kind of confused. I mean, I know he doesn't, because he loves me. But it's still kind of, I don't know, awkward or uncomfortable, just the whole situation.

Simone's confusion in this situation shows her desire to believe her brother would never think racist thoughts because his sister is Black, and shows her discomfort with considering the possibility. Even within the same family, different caste positions are represented, and will interact in ways that are sometimes unexpected by adoptees.

For Sadie, who was raised by her grandmother, who is White, an awareness of bias has developed, but Sadie has concluded that, "She's not racist, but she does sometimes say biased things." She added part of her parent's personal history to support her assertion: "Because I know in high school, she used to get in trouble for hanging out with Black people. So, I know she's never been a super biased type of person. It happens sometimes. I feel like that happens to everybody." In the end, Sadie accepts that they have different views, stating, "Sometimes she just has that kind of opinion, though I can't really think that or say that, but it's all you."

This acceptance of some family members who hold archaic ideas related to race was also shared by Kaitlyn in reference to a grandparent. She wrote the following passage in a journal entry:

> My great grandma is 83 and she grew up back when Black people were called colored people. That doesn't really bother me because she's old and is just saying what she is used to. She also said to me that she is tired of hearing how much harder the Black man has it than the White man because each person has the same amount of problems. I don't argue with her when she says these kinds of things because she doesn't get out much and she doesn't watch the news or anything to see what's going on in the media. She may say things like this sometimes because she really doesn't know what is going on, so I don't even get mad.

Kaitlyn understood her grandmother's perspectives within a historical context that helped her see the reasons for her grandmother's limitations of awareness related to race.

Another way that gratitude for family showed itself in participant stories was the when a parent advocated for and protected participants. In one story, shared by Alyson in a journal entry, she had been stopped by a White man while walking in her own neighborhood. Her presence in the community was questioned, and the man told her it was private property and she was trespassing. She wrote:

> He continued to badger me with questions until I answered his specific questions like what my exact address was and making me point to exactly where I live before he left me alone. There were other people walking around the neighborhood at that time, there always were. The difference . . . they were White. A week later, the same thing happened to me while I was walking in my neighborhood with my partner Logan, but by a different man who was walking his dog. We immediately went home and this time, my dad was home and I told him what had occurred. What would happen next, truly changed my adult life in how I came to realize how much my dad actually does care about me. I don't know if his understanding of race and racism culminated at this point but it sure seemed like real life racism hit him all at once. He grabbed his jacket and his shoes and marched out the door and found the man I described to him standing in his driveway some houses down the street. My dad confronted him and told him to stop harassing his family and to leave his family alone and that it is not a crime to walk around the neighborhood. He told the man that if he ever bothered his family again, that he would report him to the authorities. I . . . will. . . . never . . . forget . . . this. This is the first time my dad EVER confronted anyone. The first time I have ever seen my dad stand up for me, or anyone, really. And it made so much sense. . . . he dealt with this the same way he has dealt with everything

> else in our life, not by dialoguing with me or talking about it or sharing emotions but rather taking direct action as a result of his love for me.

This event was clearly meaningful for Alyson, and it caused her to feel a deeper understanding of her father as a person, and also a deeper understanding of the loyalty and allegiance between her and her dad. For the first time, she could feel that they were on the same side, with a shared understanding that injustice had occurred. Kaitlyn made a statement during her interview that summarized how handling difficulties together can bond a family together. She said, "I think sometimes you have to go through rough times to realize that the family you were put in is the family that loves you the most."

Chapter 6

The Political is Personal

The following segment of a spoken word poem by Alyson introduces chapter five: The Political is Personal.

> She told me affirmative action is the only reason I got in
> Not knowing that my application was stronger than hers to begin [with]
> Not knowing that without affirmation of our black and brown skin
> That the racist policies and people still wouldn't let us in
> Constantly questioned about my own intelligence
> Does not help the bias, you are convinced doesn't exist
> Deflection of my feelings and lived realities
> Does not properly reflect your so-called empathy
> I want to understand you, I promise - I do
> But I just wish you would try to take a walk in my shoes
> I was told my gorilla nose don't belong here
> I was told I need to tame my wild and curly hair
> Oh and your minority scholarships are just so unfair
> But what they failed to see, is we breathe the same air . . .

This chapter demonstrates the personal relevance of racial politics in the lives of participants. For the generation coming into emerging adulthood at this time, racial politics are more visible than ever before. Social media and hand-held phones record and spread news quickly. Participants share a range of insights, stories, and viewpoints in this theme, illustrating further how participants are experiencing and understanding race as they move through emerging adulthood.

Many participants discussed events related to the 2016 United Stated presidential election in their interviews and journal entries. The election had clear relevance for participants as people of color in the United States. Emilie shared, "I got to a point after the election where every White person was the enemy, and it's taken me some time to sort of get to a place where I believe that maybe we'll be okay." Simone discussed what it was like to see campaign logos on friends' social media accounts. She talked about how this caused her to think about friendships in a different light. She stated:

> But I'm like, are all my friends racist? Because they're supporting him. He talks bad about minorities, women, people with disabilities. So, I have a tough time getting behind someone like that. It definitely opened my eyes, because if they support him, they share the same views. To some extent, they do. So, I just kind of like distanced myself from a lot of the people on Facebook or a lot of my friends because I don't support him at all. But I'm like, "now I don't really know if I'm your friend."

In a journal entry, Cherise remembered the election and what it was like to attend class at the university the day that Donald Trump won. She wrote:

> I remember when Trump first became "president." I was on the phone with my friend waiting in anticipation. I remember her crying because her mom was an undocumented immigrant and Trump's viewpoint of them was incorrect and unforgiving. I think at that point I knew that was a clear indication as to where we were as a country. The election was made up of votes of mostly White women. I remember having to go to class in defeat that day and how it was especially difficult because I was at a predominately White Christian college. Many of these people were republicans and I tried to not feel a slight disdain for my peers. When Trump became president for many of my peers it was just another day. But I knew my rights as a queer Black woman would be threatened and things would certainly be different.

Sadie shared her point of view related to racial progress. She wrote in a journal entry, "It seems as though we've made progress with race and acceptance and equality, but if you ask me, we are at the point where we are at a standstill and are kind of going backwards." She continued, writing about how she feels limited in terms of traveling or deciding where to live:

> It is kind of a scary thought, though. The fact that there are people out there so passionately racist, and active about it. It is so bad in the world that there are certain places I don't ever want to go. I used to want to move to Alabama, but that is a scary thought now. You couldn't pay me enough to go to Mississippi, and I am planning on moving to Atlanta after college, and now that is even scary. I just think it is sad that people have to still live in some type of fear just because of the way that they look.

While Kaitlyn did not discuss traveling, she did mention her feelings about the place she grew up, and her family's experiences with the local police:

> I think they were targeting our family more than the other houses. Because, like, some of the houses would deal drugs, but they would never go in there. But if we got too loud or like—my dad and my brother were arguing. They'd always be knocking at our door. The police didn't really like our family, and I think part of the reason was because of our diversities. So, I think we were kind of watched a little more than the other families. My parents have Black children, so they don't like it.

Kaitlyn explained that she and her family members were visibly in support of Black causes. She shared that her dad chose to kneel at her soccer games in support of peaceful protest against police brutality against Black people. She shared, "My dad used to kneel at my soccer games, but I asked him not to because no one else was, and I was kind of embarrassed. But he supports that. And me and my brother support that too. We all support "Black Lives Matter."

Maryama shared in her interview how her awareness of Black culture and history was related to her awareness of racial politics. She said, "I feel more defensive or supportive for my Black community. Back then, I really didn't care. But now, I understand the struggle, the culture and the background." Jacob also mentioned that studying Black history was influential in seeing how racial politics could affect him personally. He said, "It helped me to better contextualize racism in the United States. And I think that brought me into a feeling of, wow, I really need to learn a lot more about like, what's going on and how it affects me as an African American male." These stories of adoptees' growing awareness of Black history due to self-motivated study points strongly to the lack of such information and conversations during their education in mostly White spaces. Emerging adulthood brought a new freedom to access information relevant to their racial identities; information that was not provided previously in their lives by schools or by parents and family.

Austin talked about his process of becoming an activist starting in college, and how this influenced his feelings about the personal relevance of racial politics. He stated:

> I was very apolitical for most of my life. But I went to college. I went to a liberal arts college and began to sort of grow my understanding and, the seeds of my activism were planted. Gradually, I became so militant in many ways that I lost a lot of friends. I became very vocal. And, it was very much so, "You either give a shit or you don't. And, if you don't give a shit, you don't give a shit about me, then. And I don't want you in my life." I lost friends. I would get into fights with friends over things, screaming matches over the world. And I don't regret a single moment of it, to be very clear.

Austin continued, discussing how his personal relationship life was related to racial politics. He said, "I met the man who would eventually become my husband. He's a very political man. If I thought that I was becoming political in college because I went to some rallies, that was nothing compared to dating a man who had been a field organizer for President Obama." When Austin and his now husband were planning their wedding, they planned to have voter registration cards for guests. His mom did not support of this idea and told him he could not have them. When Austin asked what she meant, his mother said, "You don't mix the personal with the political." Austin's response to her was, "Mom, I'm marrying another man. And the only reason that's legally recognized is because of politics and field organizing. So, my life is political. I'm a gay Black man. My life is political."

Participants noted the presence of racial politics in most arenas of their lives during interviews and in journal entries. For example, Alyson wrote about medical school:

> Based on my experiences as one of the few people of color in medical school, I have a lot of built up anger and things I'd like to explain to my White classmates. It deeply saddens me that many of them display a huge capacity of intelligence to learn the biomedical sciences, but lack common empathy and understanding of the experiences and/or history of Black people in America. It pains me to know they will be doctors next year who will have patients that look like me. Based on many people in my classes' comments, how they view the world, their lack of desire to engage in cultural competency experiences, and their disdain that they project upon anything that threatens their privilege, I would venture to regretfully say that they will project some serious bias in their future practice and further contribute to the ethnic and racial health disparities we have today. When social injustice occurs right in front of their eyes, their silence is deafening. I just wish they would take the time to listen to the experiences of people different from them and just believe us, instead of questioning everything and getting so defensive.

The personal relevance of racial politics is further explored through two subthemes: (a) My Eyes Were Opened and (b) Divide in Family over Racial Politics.

MY EYES WERE OPENED

Participants shared stories and thoughts related to personally experiencing feeling "othered" or "less than" because of having an oppressed racial identity in a racialized society. Participants shared experiences of stereotype threat, microaggressions, incidents of racism, and coming to a greater understanding of systemic dynamics related to race, all of which had a part in participants seeing the political as personal. For transracially adopted emerging adults, the realization of oppressed identity based on experience is a unique aspect of the Political is Personal. Without the influence of Black family members and the absence of experiences like watching one's parents, siblings and extended family and neighbors coping with oppressive circumstances, some participants came to the realization and understanding of oppressed racial identity during emerging adulthood rather than during childhood or as an inherited culturally socialized fact of existence. For some participants, the realization was in retrospect, when knowledge and language related to race and racism gained in emerging adulthood provided a lens through which participants could interpret their earlier experiences with greater understanding.

In a story told by Cherise in a journal entry, she shared about the first time, at 19 years old, that she experienced being treated as if she were a threat because of the color of her skin. She wrote:

> I was waiting for my Uber to pick me up and I was sitting in front of 7-Eleven when a lady working there comes out. She tells me that I'm not allowed to sit in front of the store because I was making one of the customers inside uncomfortable by standing in front of her car. The lady was apologetic but said to me "You know how it is." And I just remember thinking, "No, I really don't." Me being very unconfrontational, I agreed to move to the side of the store. I was doing nothing wrong and strongest emotion I felt at that time was anger. Anger because she didn't even know me, anger because I was so docile about the whole situation. I wish I would have stood up for myself and told them I was doing nothing wrong. That was the first time that I'd ever really experienced somebody seeing my skin and thinking that I was a threat.

In a journal entry, Alyson explored this idea of stereotype threat. She wrote a list of examples from her life:

> Do you know how many times I have . . .
>
> > . . . stayed silent in my life in fear of being the Black girl who always brings up issues?
> >
> > . . . tipped too generously despite horrible service in fear of being the Black people who don't leave good tips?
> >
> > . . . been overly pleasant and apologetic even when I have been disrespected and walked on just to avoid being labeled as the angry Black girl?

> . . . dimmed my light or decreased my self-worth so others can feel better about themselves so they don't get jealous of me?
>
> . . . ran slower in a track race or sprint at basketball practice just so they wouldn't think I'm just fast cuz I'm Black, despite me working 10 times harder on a daily basis?
>
> . . . not raised my hand in class when I knew the answer as to not outshine the white people and have them resent or fear me?
>
> . . . withheld the fact that my parents are white so that they don't say, "oh that makes sense, we knew the only reason a proper Black like you made it was cuz them white folks raised ya"
>
> How many times you ask? TOO MANY

Maryama shared her reaction to experiencing racial microaggressions, stating, "I would always have White people say, 'Can I touch your hair?' Oh, I hate that. I still hate it today. People put their hand on top of my head, and I'm like, 'Please stop. Like, please don't do that.'" Microaggressions were a part of Sadie's story as well. She shared the following story about her experiences at work and school in a journal entry:

> One time this older White guy told one of the other black cashiers that he didn't know 'colored' people worked here. I actually really hate the word 'colored' as a way to describe skin color, because every time I think of like the segregated 1960s, and it makes my skin crawl. I feel awkward and out of place working there. I feel like I am always looked down at like I don't know what I am doing. Even at the school of music, there are not a lot of music majors that are Black, so I feel like when I walk down the halls, I have to prove myself more than everyone else. I really hate sometimes that skin color is something that makes you automatically look weak and inferior. I want to prove myself but based on my skills not my appearance.

Several participants wrote and spoke about being in mostly White spaces, and how they began to have a different perspective in those spaces. In a journal entry, Emilie shared a story that caused her to realize her unique position as a biracial woman in White spaces. She wrote:

> When I was a senior in college we were beginning to grow apart, but the final straw was at a Friendsgiving dinner where we were all drinking and having a fine time, until one of the guys, [de-identified], who is White, said "Let's listen to some nigger music." I had never heard him say anything like that before and I'm honestly not sure where it came from or where he found the audacity to

> say nigger in my presence and expect nothing would come of it. I admittedly caused a whole scene, but to this day I feel justified because not only would he not admit he was wrong, but none of my "friends" would stand up to him with me. It was in that moment that I realized that in my life, as a person with my background, privilege, and complexion, I have a very simple choice around white people. I can either sit back and let things happen to fit in and not cause waves, or I can stand up for what I believe is right. Unfortunately, I also realized that day that many people will expect me to sit back and shut up in the face of oppression and racism because of my complexion, and that when they realize I am unwilling to do so I find their surprise often turns to anger and resentment.

Austin considered his intersected identities, and noticed that he experiences race as a more taboo topic than sexual orientation. He stated:

> If I said my family's homophobic or if I was telling people that I was distancing myself because my family doesn't support me being gay, or doesn't accept me for being gay, or doesn't, you know, affirm me for being gay, I would be a fucking hero. I would be the bravest person in the world. But, because it's race and race is the most taboo topic, people don't want to believe that this pleasant White family that raised this well-spoken, well-educated, seemingly well-adapted Black person could possibly be racist.

This aspect of the transracial adoptive experience mentioned by Austin is inherent in many participant stories; the uniqueness of being in a family where both oppressed and privileged statuses related to race are present. This dynamic is imperative to understand, because it is in these dynamics that the historically inherited perspectives of people in privileged groups show up in the daily lives of transracial adoptees, and cause them to feel the reality of their oppressed status with family members. In thinking back about her journey of racial awareness, Cherise talked about how she began to feel strong emotions in response to police violence against Black people, and how this internal struggle impacted conversations with her father and increased her understanding of systemic and personal dynamics related to race. She shared:

> I do remember a Black male being fatally shot and it being all over the news. I remember feeling this anger, this sadness. I remember talking to my dad about it. He tried to justify police actions, as if this Black man deserved to die. I think from there that's when me and my dad started having real conversations about politics, well, more like arguments. That's when I started realizing how race determines everything. I did start to realize that my skin color does matter, you know, the way I'm perceived, the way I am treated, and just actually how important it is to me, being a Black woman.

Kaitlyn had been raised in a racially diverse area. She shared experiences related to race, experiencing racism, and understanding that she and her brother were treated differently at school, and that her family was targeted by police due to race. When she reached emerging adulthood, she encountered a new aspect of race and society: segregated Greek life on her college campus. She shared that at a Greek life festival on campus that was meant to be an opportunity for students to learn more about Greek organizations, the Black and White sororities were divided by a curtain.

So, I went to the other [White] side first to see what it was like, and they just sort of were being fake because they felt like I should just be on the other side of the curtain, but I just wanted to see what it was like. So, after that conversation, I went to the other [Black] side, and I thought that it would just be better to join one of those because no one would look at me weird or anything.

When asked what it was like for her to experience this, she shared her way of coping with racism and stereotype threat, saying, "You just sort of have to let it go. You can't just dwell on that stuff. You just have to let that stuff go because they're the ignorant ones."

Only one participant, Jacob, expressed that he did not notice being treated differently due to race. He said, "I don't really often like, notice any, I suppose, microaggressions or indicators of racism in my direction. I can't think of any scenario where that's happened to me before." He also shared a self-reflection, wondering if he didn't pick up on things other people of color might. He stated, "I don't typically analyze my interactions with people that much for hints of like, racism or something along those lines. But I know people that do. I think either I'm not informed enough to look for it, or I just ignore it and assume that it's just an idiosyncrasy of the way the person is trying to act."

Some instances of division related to political issues that felt personal to adoptees occurred within the family, which is explored next.

DIVIDE IN FAMILY OVER RACIAL POLITICS

This section contains stories of division between participants and their families due to race and racial politics. This aspect of the Political is Personal is a unique piece of transracial adoption. The personal relevance of racial politics coupled with the family tension and divide regarding racial politics adds a dimension to racial identity that is unlikely for Black emerging adults raised in Black families. Research focused on Black racial socialization reveals that messages and modeling related to blackness are meant to instill racial pride, high self-esteem, and resilience in the face of racial barriers and stereotyping

(Hughes et al., 2006). Lesane-Brown (2006) further describes Black parents as a protective buffer between racism in the world and their children. Black parents serve as a buffer by transmitting messages that help prepare their children from the racism and discrimination they will face in society. According to Brown and Lesane-Brown (2006), Black parents are primary influences in terms of educating Black children about the implications of being Black in the United States. Transracially adopted emerging adults went without this influence of Black parents. Emerging adulthood was discussed as an important time for participants to begin to understand the importance of their racial identity, what it meant in the world, and what it meant in their families.

Grotevant et al. (2000) name three aspects of identity that are salient for all adoptees: (a) intrapsychic, (b) family relationships, and (c) the social world beyond the family. In the case of transracial adoption in the United States, the social world is racialized and carries a long history of racialized oppression. Because the family is steeped in that social world, it would follow that those same racialized dynamics are present in transracial adoptive families, even if unconsciously.

In general, participants felt that some parents and family members simply did not understand the significance of race for participants, and some noticed anti-Black political views within the family. Participants recounted conversations or experiences with family related to elections, leaving participants with realizations about their family's views. Cherise succinctly stated, "Being pro-black in the eyes of my father meant that I hated all White people. But really, it had set me free."

Simone told the following story in her interview:

> Aunts, cousins, and my uncles didn't talk to me for six months. And I didn't understand because I wasn't like, yelling or anything. I just said, "I don't really support him [Trump]." And then they were like, "Well, that's racism because you"—And I was like, "How is it racism? Reverse racism doesn't really work." And that made them even angrier. It was just crazy, because I'm like, you guys didn't want a Black President. Because like when people run for President, they always drag up old issues and stuff. Like they couldn't find Obama's birth certificate. And that's how my aunts and uncles—I remember (them?) actually saying all that stuff. And I was like, is it because of that or is it because he's Black? And then like this past election, I'm like, oh, it really was because he was Black.

Maryama also shared that her family supported the Republican party when Barack Obama was running for president, and she was figuring out her own beliefs and opinions:

> So, my parents are Republican, and I remember when Obama was running. My parents formed this thing in my head, like, he's a bad guy. So, I was thinking

> like, "Okay. Anybody who supports Obama is bad." But then, in school, people were like, "Yes! First Black President." You know, all this stuff, and he stood for Obamacare. And, I'm like okay. I didn't understand the whole political aspect of it because I wasn't knowledgeable on those topics, but I was like, yeah, why not have a first Black President, you know. And then, I started wondering about why wouldn't my parents want that? They had different views because of their background, but I didn't understand that. But I never really talked to my parents about it. I'm like, okay, I support Obama as the first Black President.

Racial politics and racial identity development seemed intertwined for Emilie. In her interview she talked about how growth in her Black identity fueled a change in her political stance, making it feel like more was at stake for her personally, but she never explained that to her mom. She stated:

> I don't know that she knew exactly why I was changing the way that I was interacting with her and other people, but I think that that was one of the ways that it most manifested in our relationship was that our political differences became, sort of, like, a breaking point of our relationship. Like, we had gotten to a point where we couldn't even talk about politics in even the most remote of ways without it becoming an argument. So, we just said we're not going to talk about this anymore.

Another aspect of a divide in family over racial politics mentioned by participants was police brutality. Jacob explained that he and his parents are on opposite sides when looking at a police shooting. He shared, "They're more conservative than I am. And I'm on the opposite side. I'm way more liberal than they are. But when it comes to race, typically we don't always see eye to eye. And my dad thinks of like, police shootings as more-so like, officers attempting to do their job as best as they can verses what they really are, oftentimes."

For Austin, the issue of police violence against Black people is an area of conflict with family. He told the following story during his interview:

> And, you know, my mom, being an asshole, is talking about how hard it is to be a police officer. Yeah. This is my life. She's talking about how hard it is to be a police officer. And then, we were talking about Tamir Rice, and I said, "You know, that man murdered a 12-year-old." So, my mom's like, "they didn't murder him." At that point, I looked at [husband] and said, "We have to go. We're done now."

Another point of view was shared by Simone, who expressed that she copes with issues of racial politics by trying to see both sides. She stated, "When I discuss situations like this with my family, they often side with law enforcement. But my friends and other people my age question the polices true intentions. I like to see both sides of the situation, make a smart and fair decision or opinion."

Kaitlyn shared during her interview that she doesn't have a close relationship with family members who don't understand issues of race or who express racist views. She shared:

> My grandma, like my dad's mom, she posted on Facebook one time, it was a joke about Black people picking cotton in the fields. My brother, he wouldn't go to her house for Thanksgiving or Christmas for like three years. I still went because I liked seeing my cousin, but like I was pretty mad at her for a while, and we still don't have that tight of a relationship because of that. Because I just think that she's ignorant and oblivious to all that stuff. Like, when my dad addressed her about it, she was like, "Oh, I thought it was funny, and I didn't know that it was wrong." That just made me mad at her. And instead of calling me and apologizing to me, she just—like posted something on Facebook about it to where everyone could see it. Because I don't—I don't think she realized that that was ever wrong. I think that because like she grew up in the country with all White people, who were also kind of racist.

Sadie noticed that her White grandmother, who adopted and raised her, held on to some biased views related to race. She shared, "She always watches Family Feud with Steve Harvey hosting, and she always thinks that they give it to the Black family to win. She always thinks that and I'm like, you can't just think that, you can't just say that." When asked if she ever said anything to her grandmother about these things, Sadie stated, "Sometimes I do but it's always going to end up the same way and I leave. It doesn't really bother me I'm just like, you can't really do that."

There were some descriptions of family dynamics shared by participants that included a contradiction where the family members were saying they were open to a discussion, yet openness wasn't what participants experienced during interactions. An example was shared by Maryama. She said, "They say they're open, but they're ready to come back with any type of argument to defend their side. They always ask me, "Well, explain this to me." And, when I explain it, they fight back, and I'm like, "Whoa. I'm learning too. I'm trying to teach you. But you can't come at me like that."

Alyson shared that she often feels that she is in a position of having to defend her views with her father and feels she must prepare for conversations ahead of time so that she is ready with evidence to support what she is saying. She wrote the following passage in a journal entry:

> It is hard to change my dad's opinion of something. He prides himself in being logical and having a fixed view of how the world operates because he is well read. If he is so well read then he would understand real history and perspective,

> but he doesn't. He takes things matter-of-factly when I need him to empathize with the real-life experiences behind it because it's part of his daughter. When I made him watch my lecture on social inequity in healthcare he said "yeah all that makes sense" as if he already knew all of it and was unimpressed . . . but the next words out of his mouth are questioning a certain study or saying "I think the only way to know if this is true is if they studied [this] and controlled for [that]." These types of responses make me want to cry because I try to send my dad articles or talk to him about a controversial topic that I identify with and try to present the best evidence and logic for my truth but he always finds some way to question it, not fully accept it, or deny it with something I just don't have a comeback for. When he does this, he challenges my existence and my truth and invalidates me. It's like I'm playing this endless game of "hey I exist, see me, see us, see what you have been ignoring for decades . . . "

The political is personal was a realization for participants as race and their racialized identities became more salient for them in emerging adulthood. As transracial adoptees, this realization came later in development than for most Black people raised in Black families and communities. This experience came with the stark recognition that the racialized history of the United States is something they will have to face and navigate in daily life out in the world and in their own families.

Chapter 7

This Is Me

Research focused on racial identity and transracial adoption gives a complex and varied picture of how growing up with White parents might affect a Black person throughout life. Experiences shared by participants featured in this book continue that narrative of complexity. This chapter provides vignettes showing how experiences within the phenomenon of transracial adoption, both challenging and positive, have formed adoptees into the people they are today. Each one, in their own way, acknowledged the unique struggle related to race for transracial adoptees in emerging adulthood and also the gifts in the experience.

Alyson wrote in a journal entry that her experiences related to race as a transracial adoptee have helped her in specific ways. She related this to childhood when her birth mother told stories of her birth family's history. She explained how as she came into her own identity in emerging adulthood, her relationship to these stories changed. She wrote:

> These moments when I learned more about my origin and history are some of the most vivid and emotionally satisfying moments and pieces of information that I have ever received. I cling to these moments because it is feels like my truth, even though now in adulthood I am learning that I write my truth, not the people who birthed me. Growing up, this was all I had to quench my thirst to know where I came from and feed my identity and I hung on to it for dear life. Now, as I grow into the identity I have created for myself after years of being in one long-term identity crisis, I am slowly giving back those pieces of my story she gave me, because I don't need it like I thought I did. I now take responsibility for my identity of my late 20s rather than yearning for someone else to give me one.

Sadie shared, too, that her experiences have not been in vain. She stated, "I think that the experiences that I have had that pertain to race have helped me become the person that I am today, just for the simple fact that now I have an identity, and now I walk around with more confidence in my skin, despite the bad experiences I've had."

For Alyson, her unique experiences as a transracial adoptee, moving in different "worlds," have played a role in her professional development as a future doctor with a focus on health disparities based on systemic inequalities. She stated:

> Even though I identify as Black, I feel like I can connect with everyone. And it is my purpose to do that. It's my purpose to bring all types of understanding and perspectives and experiences together to advocate for Black people and other oppressed people and people in poverty. Anyone who's, like, the underdog, I just feel like I'm standing on the shoulders of giants who are my distant and close ancestors and everything that they have overcome to just carry that torch forward.

In considering how transracial adoption has impacted her life, Kaitlyn reflected on a poem that has held meaning for her. It is titled, *Two Kinds of Love*, and expresses how the adopted child has two different mothers that give two different kinds of love. She wrote about how this poem directly applies to her own life and her feelings about her birth mother and her adoptive family. She wrote:

> I have just always loved the ending of the poem because it always reminded me that my birth mom did what she had to do for a reason and that she is part of the reason I am living the life I have with supportive and loving parents. She is also part of the reason I have such high goals and aspirations because if I ever do get a chance to meet her and she sees the things that I have accomplished she will know that she made the right decision and my life is good because of the choice she made to give me up for a better life.

Moving through life with intersecting identities and learning more history about those identities has become a source of strength and solidarity for some participants. Cherise shared about the relationship between the personal expression of her identities in emerging adulthood and historical activist movements, stating:

> Learning my history, like queer history . . . and how it wouldn't be the way that it is now if it wasn't for women of color and trans Black women and trans women of color. I have been educating myself about and realizing that queer women of color, we're the backbone of the way that things are today. And then, also coming into being comfortable in my skin, and also being a gay woman. I think the two intersect a lot. Because if somebody were to ask me to identify, yeah, I'm a queer Black woman. I'm super proud of both of those things now.

Maryama also expressed the relationship between her intersecting identities as an important piece of her feeling of self in emerging adulthood. She stated:

> Since I've become more comfortable with my sexuality, I can be more comfortable with my race and as well as my background. I have come a long way since my freshman year in college when it comes to self-identity and me being confident in who I am. I'm still working on it, but I've made a big jump in progress, and I hope to keep continuing this progress.

For some participants, a daily continuing feeling of uncertainty is related to racial identity rooted in the unique experience of having been transracially adopted and raised in a mostly White environment. The following passage, shared by Emilie speaks to this:

> These days I still struggle with knowing where I fit in. As a light skinned Biracial woman who is often viewed as White passing or racially ambiguous, I understand my privilege in society and everyday interactions and systems, but that privilege makes it no less difficult to sort out my own identity. I do believe if I had continued to go to diverse schools and live in diverse communities, I might have a better handle on who I am, but I will never know for sure.

Simone expressed that part of what she learned from her experiences related to race is that it is okay to not be okay, and to get needed support. She stated:

> There have been times when I've been stereotyped or had something rude said to me and just needed to lay down and cry. There's absolutely nothing wrong with admitting you need help or seeking therapy or just venting to someone. Keeping things inside is not good for you, or your health. I have battled depression; I have had suicidal thoughts, but I am here today. Every day I think about how I made it to that day and am grateful.

Jacob, who is in his first year of college, said he is just beginning his journey related to racial awareness and understanding his racial identity. He wrote in his final journal entry about participating in this research study, stating, "Participating in this research study has impacted me in an extremely positive way as it has pushed me to reach further out of my personal bubble and further develop connections with people of color on my campus. It has also spurred me to continue developing my cultural awareness."

An important part of Austin's journey has been gathering his community and family of choice so that he can relax into the support he needs in daily life. He stated, "I'm very glad that I got to the point where I found the people that I need to teach me how to love myself and love my blackness."

The participants shared a diverse range of present understandings of self that are related to racial experiences as transracial adoptees. The theme of *This Is Me* is expanded in the following sections through the subthemes (a) Seeing What I Needed and Didn't Get, (b) Worldview and Perspective Related to Race, and (c) What My Blackness Means to Me Now.

SEEING WHAT I NEEDED AND DIDN'T GET

Participants articulated what they needed as racial beings and didn't get from families or environments as transracial adoptees. The awareness of what was missing and its impact on participants is an important part of understanding the experiences of transracial adoptees.

For Emilie, who is 24 years old, the realization that something had been missing didn't come to her until emerging adulthood. She stated in her interview, "Only in my later years have I really felt like I missed out on something, and maybe it's because I didn't have that diverse experience from sixth grade onward. Maybe if I had, I wouldn't feel as disconnected from Black culture as I do and that part of my identity and my blackness." This statement fits with previous research showing the importance of Black racial socialization, which remains an important missing ingredient for many transracial adoptees. DeBerry et al. (1996) describe Black racial socialization as a preparation for coping with oppression that begins as early as two years old. The racial socialization process teaches culturally relevant habits as well as values that will help children adapt in society and become competent in navigating life in a racialized society (DeBerry et al., 1996). This definition is expanded by Bentley-Edwards and Stevenson (2016) to include the transmission and acquisition of intellectual, affective, and behavioral skills with the goal of building racial efficacy. Racial efficacy allows for the reappraisal and negotiation of stressful racial/ethnic encounters. Such encounters occur within five psychosocial contexts: information and knowledge processing, relationship engagement, identity development, styles expression, and stereotype reproduction (Bentley-Edwards & Stevenson). The passing down of cultural knowledge and racial pride bolsters Black youth with internal leverage and group connection from which to draw strength in the face of racial discrimination. Because Black parents can draw from their own experiences of racial discrimination (sometimes in the presence of their children), they naturally serve as a buffer for Black children against racism in society, providing implicit and explicit messages and modeling that show Black children the meaning of being Black in the United States.

White parents are rarely included in studies of socialization about ethnicity and race, although such socialization takes place within White families, even if implicitly (Hughes et al., 2006). Because White people in the United States are part of the dominant racial group, they have the option to ignore racial identity development in themselves, and in their White children. In fact, studies have shown that many White parents do not talk openly about race, or even recognize that they have a race (Bonilla-Silva, 2014). White racial socialization differs from racial socialization in racial minority families in that White families are teaching children to navigate advantage, rather than the disadvantage inherent in the racial minority family experience (Hagerman, 2017).

Research focused on racial socialization helps build the understanding that White parents, without intentional effort and appropriate training, cannot give their Black children what they don't have to give—an understanding of racism and the experience of being a racial minority. White adoptive parents have no personal experience with surviving daily racism (Berbery & O'Brien, 2011; Samuels, 2009; Vonk, 2001). White parents might not have awareness of the systems of racism that grant them, but not their Black children, unearned privilege (Vonk, 2001). And, even with knowledge of racism and privilege, White parents might not be able to provide racial socialization in a way needed by Black children (Leslie et al., 2013). Emerging adulthood is a life phase during which Black transracial adoptees enter environments and meet people who not only raise awareness about what was missing, but also help provide some of the missed socialization opportunities due to being segregated from Black community during formative years. (More comprehensive information about racial socialization can be found in Chapter 9).

Emilie discussed how through Black people in her life recently, she has come to know more of what other Black people had for their entire lives that was just not available to her. She shared the following example:

> Throughout recent years I've also come to realize I've missed out on the larger family ties that many Black families have. My parents are older, and I have mainly been limited to my immediate family, while many Black families I know are much larger and closer than ours is. That has definitely caused some sadness for me, especially over the past few months I've gone to many family gatherings with my boyfriend, who is Black, and there are tons of extended family, with aunts and uncles and cousins and great aunts and grandparents, etc., but when he comes to visit my family it's just my immediate family. This has especially caused me to think about the stark contrast in our family dynamics.

During her interview, Sadie talked about not having been around Black people before college. When asked if she wished she that had been around more Black people growing up, she responded, "I feel like yes and no only so I wouldn't feel kind of on the outside about a lot of things. I feel like it would have helped me come to the conclusion of my culture a little more." Maryama discussed in her interview that Black people who are raised in Black families just grow up with certain things that she felt she really didn't know to ask for or about. She said, "They grow up with it, so I couldn't get that just by asking my parents, like, just going to a Black church. But, my family, they took me to African American museums. They really tried to teach me my culture, but that's the extent that they could give me. And, I appreciate them for that. I just still feel like I missed out."

Some participants shared that they did ask for certain things related to Black culture. Jacob reflected, "I can poignantly remember learning about Kwanzaa and asking my mom why we don't celebrate it. And that kind of like, culture is one of the things that I feel like I missed out on. Understanding those aspects. And being more in touch with like, who I am racially."

Representation was something mentioned by participants that was missing, as well. Cherise explained, "I wish that I had been around more proud, confident Black girls. Because it took me a long time to realize how beautiful my dark skin is. Black girls have been living their lives unapologetically Black for a long, long time but it took me a lot of learning, growing, and educating myself to realize my self-worth."

This idea was also expressed by Simone. She talked about an actress she loves to watch on a popular show, and said, "She's just like a brilliant mind. It's not even because she's an actress and she's good. She's a good person all around. Those are the Black women I wish I'd had when I was younger because there wasn't really anybody to look up to."

Language and a deeper understanding of race and racism is another thing that was missing for some participants. Alyson shared:

> I was ill prepared to know who I am in the world. We have to teach children to associate names to emotions and explore reactions to experiences. That is the language I wish my parents taught me about race, racism, and complexities of an interracial racialized society. I wouldn't have been so lost for so long. To this day I struggle to express myself and match words and feelings together about things I experience with race.

Without Black people in the family, in addition to living in a mostly White neighborhood and going to a mostly White school, it would be difficult for Black youth to form reflective relationships that would encourage racial identity development. This leaves the task of racial socialization up to adoptees, usually after reaching emerging adulthood and venturing into more diverse social and educational environments.

In addition to language and cultural experiences, learning to deal with racism was mentioned by participants. Kaitlyn shared that she would have liked to learn more, and she also came to accept that she would just have to learn as she lived life. She stated, “Definitely learning to deal with racism better, but I think that’s just something that you have to learn as you go through life, because your White parents are never going to fully understand what racism feels like. That’s just something you have to learn how to deal with it on your own.”

While Austin discussed not being taught how to deal with racism, he also shared that there was a deeper experience he missed that was more important to him. He shared, “But the thing that I’m probably the most upset about is not necessarily the lack of skills being given to me to handle discrimination. It was the support that comes from being raised by Black people specifically, for me, to love yourself for your blackness and not value and center whiteness.”

These reflections shared by participants about feeling unequipped to deal with racism and discrimination align with previous research in transracial adoption. For example, Samuels (2009) conducted a qualitative study of multiracial transracial adoptees, most of whom reported that they did not receive racial socialization messages from their parents. Additional studies report that low levels of racial socialization are linked to TRA adolescents’ feelings about racial differences, feelings about themselves, and feelings about their ability to cope with racial discrimination (Andujo, 1988; Evan B. Donaldson Institute, 2008; McRoy & Grape, 1999; McRoy & Zurcher, 1983).

Expanding the topic of what was needed and missed in the lives of transracial adoptees, two of nine participants discussed that they felt they would have benefited from stricter discipline from parents. They compared the style of discipline of their parents to their Black peers, and felt they had gotten away with too much during their teen years. Maryama reflected:

> I feel like, growing up, I got away with a lot of stuff, a lot of stuff. I was able to sweet talk my way out of things or just get away with a lot of things that a majority of African American kids could not, who got whoopins or had, what’s it called, curfews. Like, there would be times in high school that I wouldn’t come home until the next day, but my parents were like, “Well, as long as you call.” And, I remember telling my friends that. They were like, “No, I would have got beat.” Maybe it would have taught me more, not humility, but discipline? But, at the same time, I wasn’t making stupid decisions.

Alyson shared a similar idea, discussing many things she got away with, and things she did that her parents did not ever question. In retrospect, she wonders if her parents being stricter would have reduced the amount of trial and error she went through during teen years. She stated, “I got away with a lot of, like, alcohol stuff in high school that they kind of just, like, pretended not to see. And so those habits persisted through college. And I feel like I'm not good at saying no because they didn't say no to me."

WORLDVIEW AND PERSPECTIVE RELATED TO RACE

Stories shared in this section describe participants' worldviews and perspectives on race and racism. These worldviews and perspectives illustrate how the unique experience of being transracially adopted might influence emerging adulthood viewpoints about race in society.

Alyson shared her worldview on race in the form of a spoken word poem, an excerpt of which follows:

> My dream is for us to foster human connection
> Meet each other half way with love and affection
> But the reality is you are familiar with complacency
> It makes sense, because you are not the one facing Inequality
> I wish you would just say something, anything at all
> So we could stand together and break down these walls
> I wish your silence on the racism would end
> So we could all begin to heal and mend
> I wish we could march hand in hand
> With common purpose in our common land
> Freedom should be the rhythm of everyone's song
> But the country is off beat and the lyrics are wrong
> The silence is deafening, and nothing gets done
> That's why I'll be singing Black Lives Matter, until our fight is won.

This creative work presents a worldview steeped in activism, knowledge of systemic dynamics, and being a part of a movement working for a change related to racism. It is echoed by Austin, who said, "Race will forever remain a taboo topic within a white supremacist society. Even in the most 'progressive' of spaces, it's still considered radical to address those power dynamics. It's still difficult to get people to understand how to de-center whiteness and center blackness and POC identities, voices and bodies."

Cherise discussed the need to be around people who were at a similar level of understanding in terms of issues of race and social justice issues, because she has observed White people depending on people of color for education about issues of race. She shared:

> I just want to surround myself with people who are on the same level as me in terms of having the same views on Black issues and gay issues and human rights and all of that stuff. We [my partner and I] have the same exact views

> and morals. I like to obviously educate people, but I don't also think that Black people really owe White people an explanation, because that can be super exhausting. I try to have conversations with my family about it and they don't understand, I feel I have to pick and choose my battles. I feel like there's just so many more ways to educate oneself than always going to a person of color for certain things, you know? If they really wanted to educate themselves, there are books about it. I don't mind talking—But a lot of times we aren't being heard, so it gets frustrating.

Cherise's connection to a group identity with other Black people can be seen in this quote. She relates what happens to her on a personal level to what happens to Black people in general in the United States.

For Maryama, there is a definite connection between her personal development and the worldview she now holds. She shared in her interview:

> Since coming to college and being in tune with my culture and just loving myself for who I am, my hair, my figure, my background. My worldview and perspective related to race is that yes, there's problems with race today unfortunately, and I know that as an African American female I will continue to have to struggle with these differences, but I don't want people to think that it's a setback for me. Though I'm aware, that's not gonna stop me from achieving what I want.

On a different place in the spectrum in terms of worldview regarding race, Sadie shared that she disagrees with the idea that cultural appropriation should be highlighted as a transgression. She stated:

> Another thing that gets me is when people say that another group of people is 'stealing' a culture. When White people like to do stuff that typically Black people do, they are accused of "stealing a culture," and that's when people try to accuse others of trying to act like a race that they aren't. I think people should be able to act how they want to act, regardless of their race, or anyone else's race, and without being accused of trying to be something else. I think this is what starts lots of problems, because people are so worried about what everyone else is doing, and always end up bringing race into it somehow.

This perspective seems congruent for Sadie based on her personal experiences of being told she "acts White" or being told by White people that she is "trying to act Black," and not appreciating their judgment of her behavior.

Simone reflected on her experiences in a journal entry, and said that she would give her younger self a piece of advice if she could. That advice is:

> Everyone is always watching. No matter the situation or where you are, someone is watching you and how you present yourself. There have been many

> times when I have been profiled and had the chance to be irate or upset. I have to remind myself every time that how you react to these situations also contributes to people's stereotypes of minorities. At the same time, you can stand up for yourself without being the stereotypical angry Black woman people expect you to be.

Simone shared at several points in her interview, times at work when customers accused her of losing control or yelling, and she took pride in the fact that she was always able to confidently tell her boss to view the store security footage to verify that she had not raised her voice or lost her temper. She said that her parents often comment to her that she doesn't show emotion or get visibly upset. For her, this coping mechanism has been useful in avoiding association with certain stereotypes about Black people and has contributed to her perspective.

WHAT MY BLACKNESS MEANS TO ME NOW

In this aspect of the theme, *This is Me*, participants share the meaning of being Black from their unique perspective as transracial adoptees and emerging adults. It includes a range of racial identity development among participants, which helps us further understand that complexities of the individuation process are related to race for transracial adoptees. One participant expressed that his process of learning about race and his racial identity is fairly new, and when he was asked what his blackness means to him, he responded, "I don't know if it means anything really like, explicit. I think it's just like, a case label. Something that just identifies me as an individual. I don't know if it plays into any of like, my interactions as much." Sadie discussed how her Black identity is fairly new as well, but that it has played an important part in her development during her first year of college. She said:

> It makes me want to be able to just share my experiences and my knowledge. Because I think I've definitely learned a lot in the past year. I'm not the same person I was coming into college at all. A lot of that has to do with finding my identity with my race. It's a great part for me. It's a little uncomfortable thinking about being in the world looking like this and kind of having the upbringing that I did, but at the end of the day I have the power to decide how I feel and how I react.

Several participants talked about how the degree to which they feel solid in their identity is directly related to their journey of transracial adoption. Emilie described the current meaning of her blackness:

> It [my Black identity] almost feels a little artificial, if I'm being totally honest, because it's, it's something that I found only recently. I wish that it was something that I felt had deeper roots. I think that, unfortunately, being raised by White parents did take that away from me because, as much as they tried, like, there's only so much you can give a child that isn't from a place where you come from—and isn't in their daily interactions.

Expressing something similar, Alyson shared, "I think now it's [my blackness] probably overexaggerated because it's like I was White my whole life, and then just got reborn Black. So, it might be heavily exaggerated rather than someone who encompassed their blackness since birth and growing up."

Relating to the meaning of blackness not being solidified, Maryama shared the following: "I don't feel that Black power I'm supposed to feel, you know, as I'm supposed to love my identity as a Black woman. According to society, I'm supposed to identify with these other things, and I'm, like, if I don't identify with them, how am I supposed to feel that Black power as being a woman. So, I'm torn. It's an everyday battle with me sometimes."

Cherise also related to the idea of an everyday battle to maintain the mindset she chooses. She said in her interview, "It's a mindset that I have to have every day that I'm, like, 'Okay. I am worthy. I'm awesome.' I must have that mentality about, you know, that I am as good as my peers and I am intelligent, and I am valid. I have to work on and not letting certain anxieties of how I'm perceived by others and not let other people dictate what it means to be Black."

Showing a different place in the spectrum of the meaning of blackness, Austin shared that he has noticed a recent shift that has come with his choice to create distance between him and his parents/family. He explains in his final journal entry:

> Truthfully, the righteous rage that I experienced when I began to wake up has subsided. There are still flares of anger any time there is something unjust, but I don't feel it overtaking my every waking thought. There is more of a sense of peace with my identity, and I think that is largely because of the fact that I have created a family and a community that embraces and celebrates my blackness and my queerness and all of my identities. Those people have fostered a sense of hope, a sense of resiliency, a sense of pride in my blackness. Something that I never had growing up. Something that my family of origin didn't give me. So, moving away from them has been a radical act of self-care and a way of continuing to develop and strengthen my Black identity and the pride I feel from it.

Alyson has found a strong connection to her blackness through history, and through her birth father's African immigrant identity, and through her work as a physician. She shares the positive meaning her blackness has for her that includes her ancestry and a feeling of group identity:

> My blackness connects me to Africa and my ancestors' spirits. It connects me to wisdom, truth, and power. My blackness alone is a reason to move forward and to keep grinding and leave this world a better place. It is an anthem to inspire me to be my best self so that I can raise children that are empowered and healthy and conscious in order to continue the legacy of paving the way for equity and ownership. My blackness is an invitation to see every other Black person as my brother and sister and uplift them in a society that oppresses them. My blackness opens doors for me to open doors for others.

As somewhat of an outlier, Kaitlyn reported *not* struggling with her Black identity. She always lived in a diverse area and had Black people in her life, which may have contributed to this unique experience of security in her blackness. She said, "Well, I think it [my blackness] means a lot, especially since I want to find my birth mom. I think it's one of the things that defines me right now. I love everything about being Black. I think it's one of the things that makes me unique and beautiful, and I'm not really ashamed of it."

The above range of descriptions of participants' understanding of the meaning of blackness in their current lives provides a view into different ways the story of transracial adoption can influence the life journey, and the importance of emerging adulthood as a time of discovery and progress in racial identity development.

Chapter 8

Transracial Adoption and the White Racial Frame

This chapter applies the white racial frame to transracial adoption in order to help adoptees, adoptive parents, and professionals in adoption policy and research see the underlying racialized social structures affecting and influencing transracial adoption. The *white racial frame* (Feagin, 2010; 2013) is a model explaining and describing systemic racism that outlines the historical building blocks and lasting systemic constructs that maintain and perpetuate White supremacy and racism in United States culture. The white racial frame is a conditioned conceptual map that influences cognition, and filters out ideas and experiences that do not fit (Smith, Jacobson, & Juárez, 2011). When applying the white racial frame model to transracial adoption, the acknowledgment of unique racial histories that inform current relationships is vital. The white racial frame produces a social context in which White people are not encouraged to examine their whiteness, have an incomplete understanding of racialized United States history, don't have regular exposure to or accurate understanding of contemporary experiences of people of color, and enjoy an explicitly and implicitly maintained insulation by default. Because this cognitive and emotional frame is inherited, it happens automatically for most White people in the United States That means, without an intentional intervention designed to expose this frame, it will be seen as "the way things are," and, more directly, "the way I am."

The white racial frame extends literature by scholars such as Baden and Steward (2007a; 2007b); Smith, Jacobson, and Juarez (2011); and Willis (1996), who include historically rooted contemporary theory related to systemic racism, whiteness and white supremacy in transracial adoption. The inclusion of the white racial frame also acknowledges the troubled history of transracial adoption in relation to systemic racism. For example, groups such as the National Association of Black Social Workers have struggled to find institutional, equitable, and culturally respectful solutions to the systemically created problem of the disproportionate number of Black children in foster care.

Perhaps the clearest example from participant stories of the pervasiveness of the white racial frame was the story told by Austin in which he attempted to discuss how his family's racism has affected him, and his mother's first statement in the conversation was, "We raised you to be a White boy from the suburbs." This statement may seem preposterous coming from a White mother to a Black young adult, but it is probably quite honest. Without an intervention designed to expose and dismantle the influence of the white racial frame, this mother would have *nothing but* the white racial frame to use as a paradigm related to race. And in the white racial frame, only whiteness matters because whiteness is the standard against which every other racialized group is measured and assessed. So even though this woman's son was Black, she could only give him what she had—whiteness. This is not to excuse this parent from the responsibility of adjusting her paradigm to acknowledge and appropriately value her son's blackness. Rather, it is to expose the idea that without an understanding of the pervasiveness of the white racial frame and race-focused required trainings that teach White families to examine their racial paradigms, transracial adoption will simply be another cog in the wheel of white supremacy, perpetuating systemic racism. Austin's story reflects the Shireman and Johnson (1987) study in which researchers asked White parents how they wished their adopted African American children to identify racially. Only 11 parents stated they wished their child to identify with the Black race. The remaining parents wished their children to identify as White, human, or no race.

The white racial frame makes whiteness continually unnamed and unexamined. It is the invisible default, which decides thoughts, feelings, and beliefs related to race. Therefore, unless White transracial adoptive families somehow independently work to learn about the racialized history of the United States, become invested in gaining a deep and humble understanding of how they are a product of and a perpetuator of the white racial frame, seek a community of racially diverse relationships, and intentionally form a family-wide anti-racist identity, the white racial frame will continue to run much like the operating system on a computer. The operating system will determine the racial interface, choosing what is seen and how it is seen, and what will and won't be done. The white racial frame is in some ways similar to the racialized caste system described by Wilkerson (2020) in the book *Caste: The Origins of Our Discontent*. Wilkerson writes of the racialized caste system as guiding us "beyond the reaches of our awareness. It embeds into our bones an unconscious ranking of human characteristics and sets forth the rules, expectations and stereotypes that have been used to justify brutalities against entire groups within our species" (p. 4). This description of caste makes the important point that systemic racism functions unconsciously. This characteristic applies to the white racial frame as well, and serves as the rationale for applying the white racial frame directly to the stories shared by adoptees in this book.

The current study offer examples of white insulation, which is a common feature of the white racial frame. *Exposure and Representation, They Don't Get It, Communication (or Lack of) About Race, Having to Teach Family, Between Two Worlds,* and *Seeing What I needed and Didn't Get* all illustrate parents and other family members being insulated in whiteness, which prevented them from interrogating issues of race, seeking education related to race, or having an interest in race/racism, even as it related to their children. White insulation creates a paradigm in which White family members do not address race, reiterating the fact that as the dominant racial group, White people have the option to ignore racial identity development in themselves. Family members might not realize they are insulated, and that the white racial frame is at play. It is a phenomenon that adds to the burden related to race for transracial adoptees, causing them to, even at a young age, learn through trial and error about their own identities, and then be placed in the position of informant and motivator about issues of race for the family.

Research related to white racial socialization illustrates the ways that white insulation takes place in families and child rearing. Societally, advantage within a racialized caste system is seen as a positive rather than negative thing to possess, and so it would follow that many White parents would not see the reason to teach their children how to navigate having something that is seen as desirable. Missing from this equation, though, is the interconnectedness of everyone in a society. When one group has advantage, that means there is a group with disadvantage. The playing field is not equal. Holding the advantage isn't something regularly thought of as something for which one might need care and preparation, and yet, it would seem that those with more power in a society might need guidance so as not to repeat the mistakes of generations past, like the White masters who justified and rationalized enslaving an entire group of people for centuries. The unconscious and implicit "handing down" of dominance as a normal part of one's group contributes, even if unknowingly, to the perpetuation of systems of oppression. Children reared with the colorblind approach reported believing that racism is no longer a problem in the United States, and that they had no advantages as a White person in this country (Hagerman, 2014). The danger of colorblind ideology is the idea that race no longer matters (Hagerman, 2017). This perspective effectively erases the discriminatory experiences of people of color in the United States, and brings the risk of victim-blaming people of color for their position in the racial hierarchy. Adding transracial adoption to the equation introduces the potential for White children conditioned in a colorblind perspective to grow up and potentially adopt Black children, leading to scenarios like those described by adoptees in this book.

Part of the white racial frame is the perpetuation of White standards of beauty, and White characteristics being seen as "normal." The section in Chapter one titled, *The Hair Journey*, was a salient and symbolically rich portion of adoptee narratives that highlighted the presence of the white racial frame. There was a range of effort related to hair care made by transracial adoptive parents described by participants. Some participants shared expressions of gratitude and appreciation for the extra effort made by their parents to either learn how to care for their hair or to find salons or stylists trained in caring for and styling Black or biracial hair. On the other hand, there were also stories shared of parents cutting off their children's hair because they didn't know how to care for it, and didn't take the time to learn. There were also stories shared of hair being wrongly cared for and therefore a source of teasing or even lasting chemical burns.

Symbolically, hair can be seen as a tangible extension of racial identity. When an exasperated White parent enters a salon with her Black child and asks for all of his or her hair to be cut off because she "doesn't know what to do with it," that parent is symbolically (and probably unintentionally) sending the message: I don't know what to do with your blackness, so I am going to erase it. Add to this the mostly White environments in which adoptees were raised, immersing them in the message: "You are not normal." Many participants discussed wanting straight hair or blonde hair. Some talked about feeling self-conscious on a daily basis, wondering how White peers would think about their hair styles. Some mothers were described as criticizing daughters for flat ironing or chemically straightening their hair due to the damage caused by these procedures. At the same time, with no empowering, positive representation of beautiful and proud Black people, with a school full of White peers with straight hair, and no close family or friends who were Black and well-versed in daily hair care and diversity of styles, adoptees felt an understandable need to fit in with peers at any cost and therefore didn't proudly embrace their hair during adolescence. Through the lens of the white racial frame, one could say that the denial of their hair was the denial of their own racial identity. This denial was supported in important ways by family and by environment, complicating the journey of racial identity development and racial socialization.

This leads to another aspect of the white racial frame shown in adoptee narratives - the ownership of the problem of racism. All participants described either parents or extended family members who refused to consider perspectives of adoptees regarding racism. The white racial frame ensures that White people not see racism as a White person's problem, and will usually only engage the topic when it is brought up by a person of color. And when it is brought up, the default response is usually defensiveness, attempts to prove any claims of racism to be a misunderstanding or misperception by the person of color, proposals of exceptions to what is being pointed out by the person of color, avoidance through bringing up other factors besides race that could be involved in any given incident, silence, or an emotionally fragile response that puts the focus on caring for the White person's upset about what is being discussed rather than being compassionately present to the person of color's experience (DiAngelo, 2016). Something that consistently showed itself in the stories of adoptees was the necessity for participants to gain the ability to 'hold the tension of opposites.' Many participants consistently felt that their parents and/or families were not understanding their struggles with race, did not work to educate themselves about their whiteness or racism, and sometimes invalidated or directly opposed participant viewpoints about race as Black people. Family unwillingness to oppose the white racial frame (within themselves and within circumstances) placed adoptees in the position of having to accept being frustrated and disappointed with lack of support and having to be a teacher to family members about issues of race. This meant living with and loving people who perpetuate the very real racial issues they deal with on a daily basis.

Adoptees were on their own to find ways to overcome racial differences and create a sense of belonging in their families, and they sometimes formed an extremely close bond with parents. With their family members, especially after having experienced loss of birth parents, adoptees faced the necessity of finding a way to hold these opposing experiences. This is a unique situation for transracial adoptees. For Black emerging adults in Black families, racial discord would most likely be experienced outside of the family and home—and family and home would be a source of default support and understanding when incidents related to race were discussed. Instead, adoptees have to either explore or deny their racial reality solo, while knowing that their family members are not aware of these issues.

bell hooks (2012) writes about the difference between blame and responsibility. While White parents are not to blame for the white racial frame, they have a responsibility for becoming educated about race, racism, and for how those things are impacting them and their children in the world and in the family system. People commonly view transracial adoption as "at least the kids have a home and a family that loves them." No one would argue that permanence is not important for children being adopted. At the same time, pretending that race is not a factor in transracial adoption is negligent and causes added suffering for transracial adoptees.

Chapter 9

Transracial Adoptive Parenting

This chapter is written specifically for transracial adoptive parents. In the first section is an examination of stories shared by participants that describe their level of preparation for living in the United States as Black people. This includes looking at both implicit and explicit lessons about race. The next section provides guidelines for transracial adoptive parents to improve their family's experience of transracial adoption. Lastly, transracial adoptive parent racial socialization practices and paradigms are described and applied to stories shared by adoptees.

HOW PREPARED WAS I?

One of the concerns related to transracial adoption is the variance of White parent abilities to prepare Black children for life in the United States. It is important for White adoptive parents to understand that while their children are growing up parents are the primary, and sometimes only, resource that can influence their racial reality. Roorda (2015) discusses the process by which transracial adoptees leave the protective environment of the White adoptive home to become adults in the world, and at that point race becomes a priority because they are viewed by society based on the color of their skin. Racial socialization, including lessons related to race, are the elements providing varying levels of preparation for adoptees in emerging adulthood.

Racial socialization has been defined as a developmental process by which children acquire the behaviors, perceptions, values, and attitudes of a racial group, and come to see themselves and others as members of the group (Lee, Grotevant, Hellerstedt, & Gunnar, 2006). The process of racial socialization is unique and complicated in transracial adoptive families due to White parents being products (and unconscious/unknowing perpetuators) of White racial socialization rather than Black racial socialization. Racial socialization is the process that prepares Black children and teenagers to live in the world with a Black identity. Racial socialization occurs regardless of the level of intention or awareness related to the process. In other words, even if parents ignore race due to lack of skills, awareness, knowledge or interest, clear and pervasive messages are being sent on a daily basis to children about race through experiences, environments, media, conversations, etc. Adoptees sometimes described the racial socialization received by White parents as well-intentioned, but usually coming up short in terms of providing what was needed to feel prepared for life as Black people in the United States. Many stories were shared about not knowing cultural information, having little to no familiarity with Black people, and having to learn later than most Black people how to recognize, address, and cope with racism.

In subthemes such as *Communication and Silence about Race*, *Exposure and Representation*, *the Hair Journey*, *Race Mattered*, and *Seeing What I Needed and Didn't Get*, adoptees described both helpful and harmful racial socialization experiences from their formative years. Several adoptees described living without guidance or dynamic openness related to race. They shared experiences of disconnection, confusion, anxiety, and silence related to race. Adoptees described feeling disconnected from other Black people and having difficulty understanding their own racial identities. There were exceptions to this. Kaitlyn described feeling very solid in her Black identity throughout life and feeling prepared to live life as a Black person. However, even some of Kaitlyn's stories described times when extended family members or peers lacked a connection to or understanding of her experience as a transracial adoptee. This led to some feelings of isolation for her. Positively, she felt very aware of systemic and societal racial dynamics and felt she had developed coping skills for dealing with racism throughout her life. This confidence was not shared by other adoptees in this study.

There were many ways participants described feeling unprepared for living as Black people in the United States. Austin told of his family never teaching him anything positive about his Black identity and never helping him learn to love his blackness. He also talked about feeling uncomfortable in Black spaces, like Black barber shops, and needing help from his partner in such interactions. Several participants discussed White parents ignoring race entirely. For example, Alyson shared that while she was growing up, the words *race* and *racism* were never spoken. Many adoptees shared that they lived in mostly or all-White environments, with only an occasional out of context learning experience related to Dr. King, a dance class, or a museum of racial history. Emilie, Maryama, Jacob, Sadie, and Cherise provided examples of feeling out of touch with Black peers, unable to relate due to a lack of knowledge of Black culture, including music and movies.

An inadvertent effect of White parents' racial socialization was the internalized presence of negative or stereotypical views or judgments about Black people within adoptees. There were explicit negative perspectives of Black people heard and seen by adoptees. There was also an influential absence of positive racial socialization experiences related to individual and group Black identity. With this absence, the door is left open for the white racial frame to fill in the blanks with racist defaults. For adoptees, internalized racism is unique in that a source of the negative, internalized messages about Black people was their family members and communities. Austin described hearing and seeing overtly racist messages from family members. Alyson described only seeing Black people when she visited an inner-city area where her father worked, and having stereotypes reinforced by exposure being limited to these times. Cherise, Jacob, and Sadie mentioned seeing Black people in negative ways based on stereotypes, media, and messages from peers. Adoptees felt they were not bolstered with a plethora of positive racial socialization experiences related to Blackness. Because of this, they felt late to the process of accepting their own racial identity and having positive group racial orientation.

Unfamiliarity with the Black community made encounters with Black people in teenage or emerging adulthood years very informational and pivotal for identity development. In some cases, new experiences of exposure inspired self-directed study of Black history and Black social issues. Jacob, Austin, Emilie, Maryama, Cherise, and Sadie all described early college years as a time when their exposure to Black culture increased. They each told stories of the ways they began exploring identity and the ways they felt out of place. In the section, *Having to Teach Family*, adoptees also described having knowledge and understanding of their growing racial identity and finding themselves opposed to their parents' views of Black people, racial dynamics, and racial politics. Exposure to more racially diverse environments and involvement in racially diverse communities and relationships helped adoptees challenge the negative views they had absorbed during their upbringing, and begin the process of embracing their blackness. Emerging adulthood became a time of corrective and much-needed community and peer racial socialization.

An aspect of being prepared to live in the United States as Black people includes the race lessons that adoptees remember being taught by White parents. Adoptees told stories about both implicit and explicit race lessons from parents. Examples of *implicit* race lessons include: (a) children being taken to a salon to have their hair cut off due to lack of knowledge, effort, and familiarity with caring for Black hair, (b) parents and other family members having no Black friends and never having any Black people over to their house or choosing to live in an all-White environment, (c) a child hearing a race-based threat against him on the answering machine and no one addressing it with him, and (d) a parent supporting Black Lives Matter or kneeling at a sports event in support of ending police violence against Black people. Examples of *explicit* race lessons include: (a) parents teaching their children how to behave with police or to be sure not to put their hands in pockets in a store, (b) parents explaining that the n-word is not acceptable language, (c) a relative explaining colorblind ideals of "what's inside is what matters," or similar sentiments, and (d) parents explaining the racial history of the United States and expressing shame related to their race's history. These lessons demonstrate the complex mixture of positive and negative racial socialization experiences in transracial adoption.

Stories told by participants were filled with impressions internalized by participants during childhood and teen years. Some of these were verbal, memorable exchanges, but more often it was described as having experiences that they knew meant something related to race, but they didn't yet have the language or conceptual base to interpret the situation. This was the idea for the section titled *Race Mattered*. Participants knew very early that race was a factor, that it mattered, and that there were different races in their families. It seemed that most participants were currently still in the process of digesting and forming clear understandings of their experiences related to race due to the complexity of transracial adoption, the daily relevance of race in their current lives, and continued complicated relationships with family members.

Stories shared by adoptees illustrate the salience of race in the lives of transracial adoptees throughout childhood and into emerging adulthood, and the influential role played by White parents. Experiences related to race affected individual and group racial identity development, social development, self-acceptance, feelings of connection and belonging, and perspectives about race in society. There is resilience in the stories of participants, and an understandable bond to their families and gratitude for permanence. Therefore, we can see that transracial adoption, like most things, is not all bad and not all good. Rather, it is *complex*.

The current system of foster care and adoption is informed by dynamics of power and privilege and the white racial frame. There is less recruitment of adoptive parents of color, a disproportionate number of Black children awaiting permanence through adoption, and a systemic race-based disparity in resources to pursue adoption. Because of these situations, which do need to be addressed, but will not be solved effectively for some time, transracial adoption will continue to occur. All children need and deserve a loving, permanent home. For transracial adoptive parents, knowing that race is an incredibly influential and important factor in the lives of transracial adoptees creates an ethical duty to change *how* it happens. The following recommendations are meant to help transracial adoptive parents become intentional agents providing access to culture, knowledge, experiences, community, and discourse related to race.

RECOMMENDATIONS FOR PARENTS

These guidelines are meant to build a bridge between research based on participant narratives and the practices of adoptive parents. Much like the scientist-practitioner method upon which counseling psychology is predicated, meaning is increased when academic work becomes applicable in real life. Narratives of adoptees are honored when they can influence an improvement for future generations of adoptees.

The following suggestions are made for White transracially adoptive parents as guidance toward forming a multiracial family identity: (a) Make a consistent personal investment in anti-racism, (b) Diversify your lives, (c) Find a transracial adoption support group, (d) Communicate about race regularly, (e) Examine adoption paradigm, and (f) See color, including your own.

Make a Consistent Personal Investment in Anti-Racism

I chose to situate this book within the theoretical context of the white racial frame to inspire a change that would be rooted in changing how White parents see *themselves* regarding race, and, secondarily, influencing how they see their children, and how they help their children see themselves. Transracial adoptive parents must start with a sobering look at whiteness on a personal and societal level, the perspectives that have grown from that whiteness, and the fears that arise when it is challenged. The more parents understand whiteness, the more they will be able to help transracially adopted Black children feel supported when they encounter racism, stereotype threat, and microaggressions. TRA children will be faced with White teachers who have not faced their own unconscious conditioned racism, White friends who microaggress and stereotype them, peers who chide them for not quite fitting into racial and cultural categories, and people who are generally resistant to being aware of how race impacts them on a daily basis in our racialized society. Transracially adopted emerging adults would prefer to not have needed to face such issues at home. As I read the words of participants over and over during the two years I worked on this project, I heard young people desperately wanting those closest to them to see these dynamics from a place of personal investment. I heard them longing to not have to defend their position, explain why something was hurtful, give a history lesson, or work repeatedly to make their racial identity visible and important. Transracial adoptees want their parents to care about race and racism, and to make the effort to learn about it, read about it, talk about it, wrestle with it in themselves. From this struggle, the home environment becomes a space of safety, curiosity, support, and exploration about race, racism, and racial identity development.

The white racial frame puts the onus of dismantling racism onto people who are Black, Indigenous, and people of color. But this allows White people to shirk responsibility, and to continue to see growth in racial identity as an optional interest rather than a vital and personally meaningful act. Dismantling racism begins with White people becoming humble, open, and invested enough to do the daily work of looking inside of themselves and interrogating their own response or lack of response to situations involving race. It takes effort and time, seeking information, watching documentaries, going to workshops, diversifying their lives, listening to the narratives of people of color and also of White anti-racist activists. This takes acknowledging that all people born into a racialized society have racialized identities.

Perhaps White parents begin their journey related to race with their Black children as their reason for wanting to learn. As the journey continues, though, children benefit from parents who do the important work of finding a personal investment in the work of developing an anti-racist identity. Unaddressed and denied patterns of racism impede our humanness, and that influences our lives in all ways, including how we parent. With consistent work, White TRA parents can change their lives by breaking free from inherited, archaic forms of racial understanding, and thus, make a connection with their children that is humble, genuine, and inclusive of all identities. Suggested goals for White transracial adoptive parents include independently working to learn about the racialized history of the United States and becoming invested in gaining a deep and humble understanding of how they are a product of and a perpetuator of the white racial frame and the racialized caste system of the United States. These efforts remove the burden of transracially adopted children having to teach their parents about race and racism. These efforts also create a possibility of alignment related to race, where parent and child can stand together.

For book and film recommendations to support this journey, please see appendix A.

Diversify Your Lives

It is important for White TRA parents to recognize that some racial socialization components cannot be provided by White parents directly. For example, White parents will not experience racism personally, so they will not be able to model the handling of those situations or show the thought and feeling process for personal recovery after a racist experience. They will not be able to use their own experience of facing racism on a daily basis as a wealth of experiential knowledge to prepare their children for racism in the world. Black children benefit when their White adoptive parents are aware that they cannot provide these things, and they work to change their lives in specific and intentional ways so that the needs of the child can be met.

In stories from Kaitlyn, she is clear that greater exposure to people of color had an important influence on her development. Most adoptees reported growing up in a mostly White neighborhoods and attending schools with a mostly White population. However, Kaitlyn, reported growing up in a racially diverse community and attending schools with racial diversity among the student body. Even still, this participant stated that she only had one Black teacher during her K-12 experience. Kaitlyn shared that her Godmother is Black, and that her parents were in support of Black Lives Matter and were aware of and talked about issues related to race in society for Black people. These resources in Kaitlyn's story set her apart from other adoptees in the study. For example, she described having a secure and positive Black identity, loving her blackness, and not being able remember a time when she didn't. These variations for Kaitlyn, though, did not cause her prevent struggles related to race or transracial adoption, and she, too, experienced racism within her extended family. In general, though, her experience was different due to the racial composition of her neighborhood, school, and people close to her—as well as having White parents who were aware of race and racism in society, and who worked to support anti-racist causes.

Kaitlyn's experience with more diversity in her life, anti-racist White parents, and common conversations about race in the home growing up suggest that there are some things that White parents *can* give and *should* give in order to truly meet the racial socialization needs of Black children to the best of their ability. Parents should consider the diversity of their neighborhoods, their own friend groups, and the schools their children attend. Also, parents should consider the television shows and movies they watch. Including Black representation in parents' lives is good for them and for their children, to facilitate seeing more people of color as "normal people," familiarizing themselves with cultural norms, and humanizing Black people. It is important that parents do not appropriate Black culture, but expose themselves and their children to Black culture, allowing their children to choose their own ways to express their racial identities, even if it does not mirror the ways White parents express themselves.

Another gain involved with diversifying is the influence on white parents' anti-racism journey. If white parents have never lived in a diverse neighborhood, doing so brings the values of integration into the lives of the entire family. White parents can be neighbors with people racially different from themselves, and in so doing, provide daily opportunities for facing, processing, and challenging internalized white supremacy.

Communicate About Race Regularly

Adoptees discussed a lack of communication about race as well as an awkwardness when race was discussed with their parents. Some adoptees shared that race was never discussed unless they brought it up, and for many, conflict was inherent in race discussions with parents. Part of being a multiracial family is making race a part of everyday life and a part of normal, everyday conversation. Regular discussions about race as a part of life makes the subject less taboo, and creates an openness for children and teens to discuss their experiences related to race with their parents. Some adoptees interviewed for this project chose to not share their experiences with parents in order to protect their parents or because they knew their parents would not listen openly. Children benefit when parents choose to educate themselves and engage in their own investigations around racial identity so that their listening and interacting comes from an informed and genuine place, rather than from the default white racial frame.

Discussing race from the white racial frame perspective (the unexamined mirroring of systemic racism and white supremacy) perpetuates the problem of racism *within* the homes of adoptees. This diminishes the much-needed reprieve that home should be for Black young people in the United States, who deal with race and racism every day. White adoptive parents doing their own work related to anti-racism can serve as an authentic support, buffer, and understanding advocate. Parents need to refrain from eclipsing their children's experiences by making interactions about race and racism focused on themselves or their own learning. Communication about race needs to be supportive and focused on listening, affirming the adoptee's experiences, and understanding better how a parent can be supportive. A parent may find that having a racially-aware discussion partner, who is not the child, would allow the parent a venue to express challenges or pose questions without burdening the parent-child relationship.

Helpful communication between White parents and their Black children takes humility most of all. White parents must normalize not being the expert on this aspect of their children's experience of life. They also must normalize asking for help and looking for answers so that their racial literacy grows to a place where their support will be genuinely helpful to their kids. With effort and willingness, the family communication can be expansive rather than restrictive and add to closeness between a parent and child(ren).

Examine Adoption Paradigm

Adoption is often romanticized in our society. White adoptive parents are often seen as "saviors" of kids of color, and often the focus is placed on how "lucky" the kids are to have their parents adopt them. Because of the history of racialized power dynamics in the United States, and the history of transracial adoption, the white racial frame defaults to the judgment that the placement of a Black child with a White family is a "better" place than with birth parents. This paradigm ignores the fact that adopted children will forever deal with the monumental loss of their birth families. For transracially adopted children, that loss is compounded by the loss of racially informed culture, belonging, and community. Children benefit when adoptive parents choose to come from a place that centers their children and their children's identities as primary and acknowledges the loss of birth family and culture as important. That means that parents must adjust themselves, continue learning, and change their parenting strategies based on the needs of their children. Making efforts to communicate about birth families positively and providing support to maintain contact with birth family members are a piece of this puzzle. While each family has unique circumstances that led to adoption, a child's origin story can be honored and appreciated, as well as the people who led to their existence.

Alyson told the story of having conversations with her birth mother when she was an adolescent. She expressed how important it was to hear stories of her birth family and how as she formed her own identity, she needed those stories less, even though they would always be treasured. For children who are adopted, some things are commonly unavailable that are taken for granted by people raised by birth parents. For example, knowing the story of one's birth, seeing photos of oneself as a baby, or seeing photos of one's birth mother while she was pregnant. Centering the adoption paradigm in the experiences of adoptees is an important shift away from the White savior paradigm informed by the white racial frame.

See Color, Including Your Own

Alyson shared that when she asked her mother why she and her father adopted Black children, her mother responded that "it didn't matter" to them. They just wanted children. Interestingly, this participant struggled mightily with race being something that actually didn't matter to her parents. They were avid readers and lifelong learners, yet Alyson wondered aloud in her interview about why her parents never bothered to learn anything or read anything related to race, racism, and racial politics. Alyson deals with race, her racial identity, and systemic and institutional racism as a medical student every single day, and is passionate about solving the disparities in health care based on race. For her, the position that race might "not matter" is discordant to her because it is such an essential and integral part of who she is. She needs race to matter to her parents, and she needs them to see her race, their own race, and to understand what that means.

Colorblindness is a paradigm that is often chosen by White people to avoid the topic of race, and to avoid facing conditioned racism within. They are more comfortable saying they don't see color than facing the realities of racism on a personally relevant level. Transracially adoptive parents *must* see color, including: the history of race in our society; contemporary realities faced by their children based on race; their own whiteness and the beliefs, responses, and emotions that come with whiteness in US culture; and the development of their own and their childrens' racial identities. In addition, White parents must see, acknowledge, appreciate, and truly love their childrens' color. If parents attempt to not see color, they are missing a very big part of their children. It is important for White parents of Black children to understand that the journey of anti-racist and racial identity development is one that never ends. Experiences and learning opportunities will continue to emerge as life progresses. The commitment to continue to see race, of self and adoptees, is a non-negotiable component of being a race-conscious, ethical transracial adoptive parent.

Find a Transracial Adoption Support Group

Parents should investigate transracial adoption support groups with the intention of both parents and children forming long-term friendships with other multiracial families so that adoptees and parents can feel a normalization of their experiences, friendships rooted in shared experience, and ongoing support through challenges. Each one of the adoptees in this study inquired about the other people being interviewed in the study and expressed a desire to meet them and talk with them about what they experienced. Finding a group and committing to attending would be a great way to provide much-needed connections for adoptees and their parents. Such groups can be found through foster and adoption agencies and also online.

TRANSRACIAL ADOPTIVE PARENT RACIAL SOCIALIZATION

Stories told by adoptees in this book reflect research focused on aspects of racial socialization, adoptive parental paradigms regarding race, and communication styles in multiracial families. This section explains the ways racial socialization has been approached by transracial adoptive parents, and how those paradigms connect to the stories in this book.

Looking at the purpose and method of racial socialization in Black homes helps us see the complexity of transracial adoption related to racial socialization. Black parents pass down cultural knowledge and racial pride that bolsters Black youth with internal leverage and group connection to know how to navigate life in a racialized society with an oppressed racial identity (Bentley-Edwards & Stevenson, 2016; DeBerry et al., 1996; Hughes et al., 2006; Lesane-Brown, 2006). This, more often than not, just happens as a part of living life as a Black family. Black children with Black parents see their parents deal with race and racism on a daily basis, and receive implicit and explicit messages rooted in the Black experience. This is simply something White families cannot provide because they are living the White American experience. It is vital to distinguish here that this does not mean that White transracial adoptive parents cannot offer anything to their Black children. It does mean that *without intentional effort*, the White racial paradigm will remain primary, and will be the place from which White parents give implicit and explicit messages about race. This default of the white racial frame as the paradigm for understanding and dealing with race was described by all participants in the current study in various ways.

Several past studies conceptualized the ways in which White parents approach or think about race and racism. A qualitative study by McRoy and Zurcher (1983) focused on TRA families and explored parental racial orientations and how that influenced racial identity for transracial adoptees. The racial orientations identified included Strong White Orientation, Moderate White Orientation, and Multiracial Orientation. Researchers found that children with parents with a Strong White Orientation associated less with Black people, held common stereotypical beliefs about Black people, emphasized human identity over racial identity, had mostly White friends, and dated White people. Moderate White Orientation led to parents referring to their children as mixed or part White, but they did not de-emphasize Black heritage, and some chose racially diverse schools while still living in mostly White communities. Those with Multiracial Orientations acknowledged Black heritage in their children, chose racially diverse environments, and lived in racially diverse neighborhoods.

Stories from participants in this study showed that many parents had a Strong White Orientation. One participant described parents who would fit into the Multiracial Orientation. Participants with parents demonstrating a Strong White Orientation described adopting a Strong White Orientation or a Moderate White Orientation as a result of their socialization by parents and environments. In emerging adulthood, however, participants describe a shift in their racial orientation due to greater diversity in their friend groups and environments in college, and because of increasing experiences of racism in their own lives as Black people. The participant who described her parents as having a Multiracial Orientation claimed a Multiracial Orientation and felt pleased with the amount of diversity in her life as well as her own racial identity.

There are four different strategies or perspectives from which White TRA parents approach racial socialization, according to a review of TRA literature by Lee (2003): (a) cultural assimilation, (b) enculturation, (c) racial inculcation, and (d) child choice. *Cultural assimilation* encourages adoptees to orient toward White culture. This approach can be seen in some participant stories in the current study in both active and passive ways. Some active examples are Cherise being told by her father that growing a pro-Black identity meant she hated White people, and Austin's mother told him that she "raised him to be a White boy from the suburbs." A passive example is Sadie describing being in all White environments until she arrived at college, and by default, picking up stereotypical, negative appraisals of Black people in general. Cultural assimilation is essentially the erasure of a transracial adoptee's race-based cultural identity.

Enculturation includes an active effort to expose adoptees to their birth race and culture through educational and cultural opportunities. Examples from the current study are Emilie's mother taking her to an African dance class once during childhood and Maryama's parents taking her to museums of Black history. White parents who engage in enculturation usually focus less on race as children grow up. Importantly, both participants who described the above-mentioned efforts made by parents expressed that while these efforts were made, the overall context of the home was not one of active racial awareness. Emilie in particular shared that she had no cultural context for the dance class and did not want to continue going because she didn't understand what they were doing there.

Racial inculcation describes parents proactively preparing TRA children for dealing with discrimination and racism in everyday life. Examples of this approach can be seen in the current study in explicit conversations about two topics described by several participants: (a) being taught how to behave in the presence of police, and (b) the n-word being a word that should not be said. In general, though, participants mostly described parental paradigms that did not engage consistently in racial inculcation. Most participants learned about racism and discrimination by experiencing it and figuring out how to respond on the spot.

Child choice is the final strategy described by Lee (2003). It refers to parents providing cultural and racial opportunities aligned with the child's birth culture during childhood, but then leaving any further exploration up to the child as adolescence and young adulthood approach. This might be the most accurate choice to describe parent strategies illustrated by participants in the current study. Most participants felt that they needed to rely on sources of support, information, community, and mentorship from sources other than their White families in order to get what they needed for the development of their racial identities. This is particularly true in relation to group racial identity, which, for most participants, did not begin to develop until emerging adulthood when environments became more racially diverse.

Overall, stories shared by adoptees show that it was rare for parents to use only one strategy consistently. Some parents used bits and pieces of different racial socialization paradigms and sometimes two different strategies would be at play in the same home from two different parents. It is important to acknowledge that because of the white racial frame, cultural assimilation ends up being the default strategy in the absence of an intentional effort to enact another strategy. Even parents who attempted to come from a place of racial inculcation or enculturation still came from a place of cultural assimilation in other ways. This is not meant as a criticism of individual parents or a dismissal of efforts that were made. Rather, it is a reminder of the pervasiveness of the white racial frame. Even when efforts are made, an absence of racial literacy leaves transracial adoptees without what is needed in terms of racial socialization as a whole. For example, one participant described her parents speaking openly about race and racial history and making efforts to know how to find Black hair stylists to care for her hair. She also said her mother acknowledged that she would not experience certain things that this participant would because she is White. However, racial struggle was presented by her parents as something that happened in the past, and she expressed that she usually dealt with experiences of discrimination alone because she wanted to save her parents from the pain of knowing her struggle as a Black person. In addition, this participant's extended family would not speak to her for six months because of her choice to not support Donald Trump in the 2016 US presidential election. This example shows how even when there are specific efforts toward enculturation or racial inculcation, the gravity of the white racial frame is still a factor.

Another important piece of racial socialization is that different strategies regarding race are likely to be present among immediate and extended family members. This is another unique aspect of transracial adoption. Adoptees may have parents making efforts at racial inculcation or enculturation, but grandparents and other extended family members may subscribe to cultural assimilation, colorblindness, or overt racism. Also, two parents might have different levels of awareness regarding race, leaving the adoptee wedged between one parent who might be supportive in terms of racial identity and another who is wedded to racist ideology. This shows the importance of intentional racial socialization and personal efforts on the parts of parents to address their own racial conditioning as a vital protective factor needed in TRA families.

Another aspect of racial socialization is communication about race. Orbe (1999) identifies four main ways in which multiracial families communicate about race. *Embracing the Black Experience* describes families who immerse themselves in Black culture and emphasize Black ancestry in Biracial children rather than White ancestry. Only one participant described a parent enacting this type of communication. Kaitlyn's parents intentionally lived in a racially diverse area, sent their children to racially diverse schools, had consistent close relationships with Black people, and acted in ways consistent with anti-racist activism. The benefit of this approach is that embracing the Black experience helps children who will be seen and treated as Black by society form supportive connections and identifications with the Black community. Interestingly, the only negative expressed by Kaitlyn about her parents was that her father once said that he understood what it was like to be Black because he has Black children. So, in TRA families, it is important that the embracing of the Black experience for Black children is kept distinct from appropriation of the Black experience or an incorrect assumption that proximity to an experience is the same as sharing an experience.

Assuming a common-sense approach to communicating about race favors addressing issues of race in a way that seems to make sense depending upon each situation. This approach was described by Emilie when she talked about her parents spending more time having discussions about race and preparation for bias with her brothers, who are Black rather than Biracial. Emilie described herself as coming across as racially ambiguous due to her Biracial identity, and felt that this was why her parents hardly emphasized race with her. It is important to note that this participant felt she had missed significant racial socialization and cultural community.

Another way of communicating is *advocating for a colorblind society*. This could be seen as conducive to the cultural assimilation approach to racial socialization. This approach is rooted in an idealistic belief that ignoring the social reality of race and racism is a step toward healing racism and that "Love had no color." Unfortunately, it has the effect of erasure of the narratives and experiences of people of color in a racialized society. An example from the current study of this approach being used was when Jacob's aunt, upon his realization that his skin was darker than hers, expressed that it "isn't about what's on the outside, it's about what's on the inside."

The final way of communicating about race identified by Orbe (1999) is *affirming the multiethnic experience*. In this approach, parents embrace diversity as something special, and all cultures in the family are represented and acknowledged. In the current study, some participants described efforts made by family members to enact this approach. For example, Cherise remembers her mother helping her find comfort in identifying as Black and also made efforts to learn how to care for her hair. The bigger picture is important to consider, though. This participant also grew up in an entirely White environment, attended an all-White church, and felt great anxiety about how her White peers were perceiving her hair. While some efforts were made by this participant's mother, it is clear, how important it is to acknowledge the wider, overarching paradigm of the white racial frame and how that influences the results of efforts and sometimes dissolves them.

A unique study conducted by Smith et al. (2011) analyzed interviews from both parents and children in TRA families looking for racial socialization messages given by parents to children. The white racial frame was a guiding theoretical lens for this study. One theme identified, *Celebrating diversity: Be proud of who you are and where you come from*, was reflected in the current study. C*elebrating diversity* emphasizes individual racial identity, but usually includes isolated, intermittent exposure to culture-related historical figures or events, without an immersion in or consistent connection to a racially-based cultural community. Almost all participants described feeling a lack of group racial identity through themes of *Feeling Disconnected from Black Community*, *Dealing with Monolithic Expectations of Blackness*, *Seeing What I Needed and Didn't Get*, and *Between Two Worlds*. Even in instances when parents made efforts of exposing participants to historical information or cultural experiences, it was intermittent and individually focused and not connected to a wider context of a diverse community.

Even when there is intentional effort to see and challenge the white racial frame, White parents are still White, and cannot offer the same type of socialization given by Black parents. Again, this does not mean transracial adoption is "all bad." It does help highlight the importance of White parents making race awareness, racial socialization, diversity, and anti-racism priorities in a multiracial family.

Chapter 10

A Note to Research, Adoption, and Counseling Professionals

Narratives shared in this book by transracial adoptees can be honored by hearing and learning from them and by applying what was learned to improve experiences for adoptees in the future. This chapter provides recommendations for new directions in transracial adoptive research and implications for the practices of adoption policy makers, adoption workers, and counseling psychologists.

NEW DIRECTIONS FOR TRANSRACIAL ADOPTION RESEARCH

The study that inspired this book is intended as a new direction in transracial adoption research; one that uses specific samples based on race, type of adoption, age, and geographic location. Aggregation of international and domestic adoptees, multiple generations of adoptees, varying racial identities, and vastly different geographic locations has caused TRA research to be less specific than is needed to guide interventions in training and policy. The current study utilized a hermeneutic phenomenological method to center voices of participants in the study and to let the stories told by adoptees comprise results of the study. Qualitative research is an ideal platform through which adoptee voices can be heard without distortion. In this effort, as a researcher, bracketing was essential throughout the process. I noticed points at which I could see a tendency in myself to *interpret* participant stories instead of *reporting* participant stories. I had to stop and consult and start again more than once so that I could challenge the tendency to see predetermined results in the data instead of seeing the story told by the data. As a White researcher, it was vital to apply knowledge of the white racial frame to the research process, acknowledging that there would be times I might unconsciously be guided by my whiteness. This was one reason I sought an external auditor who is Black. Her input was invaluable in that she could identify important pieces of participant stories that I missed, undervalued, or misplaced in the results. A component that may have added more to the current study that could be incorporated into future studies is a follow-up interview to learn more about how participation in the study influenced participants. The study itself may have been one of the first or even only times that participants were asked to intentionally reflect on experiences related to race. Such a reflective experience may have contributed to growth for participants in palpable ways.

I hope TRA research will continue gathering qualitative data that privileges voices of adoptees from specific racial, age and geographic categories so that a more customized understanding of the TRA experience can be gained and then applied to changes in adoptive policy, training, and parenting. Focus groups would be an informative addition to qualitative research as well, providing an interesting dynamic in data collection that would include connections between adoptees who have had potentially similar experiences with transracial adoption. In addition, focus groups would allow for conversations among adoptees without a researcher present. This would remove the component of participant reactions to interviewer identity and may lead the conversation to places only adoptees themselves would intuitively go.

Once qualitative data is amassed, quantitative research in which variables such as adoptee racial identity development and parental white racial identity development could be explored. Also, measuring levels of preparedness for dealing with racism among adoptees might be helpful as well. Studies focused on racial literacy in foster and adoptive TRA parents prior to and following a race-focused training would be helpful in gathering information about what interventions were successful in beginning the work of dismantling the white racial frame in the minds of TRA parents. Implicit bias in adoptive and foster parents would be another variable that would be illuminating in terms of the bigger picture of race in adoption and foster care. Experiences of birth parents who lost their children to foster care and adoption also needs research attention. Looking into circumstances of separation, what services were offered and not offered, as well as what barriers prevented the reunification plan might help guide future investments into family preservation. Racial literacy and implicit bias testing among social workers might be helpful to see how the white racial frame may be showing up institutionally and personally among those who are instrumental in placement decisions.

ADJUSTMENT AND SELF-ESTEEM: ADDING RACE IS ESSENTIAL

Adjustment and Self-Esteem are frequent factors studied by transracial adoption researchers. Studies such as Feigelman (2000), Shireman and Johnson (1986), and Vroegh (1997) interpret data to suggest that transracial adoptees have no worse adjustment or self-esteem than same-race adoptees. When Adjustment and self-esteem of adoptees are studied without the factor of race included, essential complexities within lives of adoptees are overlooked or ignored. As noted by Rhonda Roorda (2015) in her book, *In Their Voices: Black Americans on Transracial Adoption*, love is important in building self-esteem, but race and ethnicity matter substantially for adoptees in terms of preparation for living as adults of color in the United States. It is possible to see the resilience of participants, their ability to function and succeed in the world, and their compensatory adjustment to their unique situations. Alongside these factors, it is possible to acknowledge the pain involved in having to fight for family members to understand the personal relevance of racial politics, the hurt accompanying experiences of racial discrimination inside the family and in society, and the awkwardness of feeling out of place culturally while with people of the same-race. Stories shared by adoptees in this book show that adjustment can and does happen even while such difficulties related to race are experienced. At the same time, having to adjust to such factors on top of the usual adjustments needed on the journey to young adulthood exacerbates the situation of TRA adoptees paying for the presence of the white racial frame. TRA adoptees are charged with coping with, digesting, and making sense of the layers of their experience that their White family members are free to ignore, dismiss, or even argue against, as was illustrated by some participant stories.

Looking at studies like Vroegh causes me to pause and consider Dr. Martin Luther King Jr.'s idea of adjustment and maladjustment. In Dr. King's speech to Social Scientists in 1967 at the American Psychological Association's annual conference, he addressed the ideas of adjustment and maladjustment. Of the word maladjustment, he said, "In dealing with what the word implies you are declaring that destructive maladjustment should be destroyed. You are saying that all must seek the well-adjusted life in order to avoid neurotic and schizophrenic personalities." He continued, pointing out that there are circumstances that call for maladjustment:

> But on the other hand, I am sure that we will recognize that there are some things in our society, some things in our world, to which we should never be adjusted. There are some things concerning which we must always be maladjusted if we are to be people of good will. We must never adjust ourselves to

> racial discrimination and racial segregation. We must never adjust ourselves to religious bigotry. We must never adjust ourselves to economic conditions that take necessities from the many to give luxuries to the few. We must never adjust ourselves to the madness of militarism, and the self-defeating effects of physical violence.

If we know that race is a primary piece of the equation in life for transracially adopted people, should adoptees have to adjust to a life that does not acknowledge, enrich, and include their racial existence? When looking at adjustment outside of the definitions and priorities established by the white racial frame, the factors we explore should be rooted in ideas developed by Black, Indigenous, and People of Color who have dealt with issues of race in the United States. We must reject the conclusion that when transracially adopted people don't complain or voice difficulty related to race to the White people around them, then they have "adjusted well." This adjustment could also be a sign of resignation: a feeling that efforts to share what is happening related to race are futile or will cause more harm for the adoptee. Adoptees not voicing their discomfort could also be a result of having little to no exposure to issues of race and Black, Indigenous and People of Color. Such exposure would have helped them develop language and literacy for such conversations.

Adjustment is survival for transracial adoptees. Coming from the loss of the biological parents, the idea of loss of or abandonment by the adoptive family is a common fear for adoptees, even if unconsciously (Eldridge, 1999; Newton Verrier, 1993). Several studies that assess adjustment of adoptees look at parent-report of problems with school, behavior, dysfunction, and perceived self-esteem (Juffer & Van Ijzendoorn, 2007; Shireman & Johnson, 1986; Simon & Alstein, 1994). Others look at global assessment or overall well-being (Feigelman, 2000). In one study, adjustment was categorized as "excellent," "good," or "with difficulty" (Shireman and Johnson, 1986). Most studies aggregate samples of international, same-race, and domestic adoptees of different races. While these studies were interpreted as evidence that transracial adoptees' adjustment is similar to nonadoptees and same-race adoptees, their failure to include race as a topic of inquiry is notable. This is especially interesting considering that when Hollingsworth (1997) conducted a meta-analysis of four data sets from the Shireman and Johnson longitudinal study, she concluded that transracial adoptees had lower combined racial identity and self-esteem than nonadoptees.

Race produces an entirely additional arena in which adjustment must happen for transracial adoptees. Adoptee narratives show that regardless of the variations in how participants approach and process adjustment related to race, race is a continuously present, salient, and an influential factor for adoptees. Adoptees themselves choose how to deal with the issue of race within their families. However, even among stories that vary in terms of how participants adjust, dealing with and adjusting to factors related to race is a dominant factor in the lives of all adoptees at some point in their journey.

Austin, who had the most anger toward and estrangement from his adoptive family, shared that his sense of security in the world was gradually built during emerging adulthood through his family of choice and his life partner. This security outside the adoptive family allowed him the space to deeply consider how issues of race had impacted him negatively throughout his life and to choose more distance from his adoptive family in order to cope. Looking at this story through the lens of Dr. King's idea of adjustment would suggest that this participant was "creatively maladjusted"; he refused to adjust to input from an environment that did not acknowledge or appropriately value his blackness. His story of adjustment is more complex than looking at factors of adjustment found on measures used in other studies.

Looking at what could be considered the opposite end of the spectrum in terms of how racial adjustment is being processed, Jacob had just recently begun intentional exploration of racial identity, and he was just learning language to understand more about racial dynamics in the United States. Even though he reported feeling that transracial adoption was a good option that saved him from some of the struggles that many of his racial peers have experienced, he still reported feelings of awkwardness and difficulty with his parents' denial of social issues of race. He also discussed an overwhelming desire to fit in with his racial peers paired with extreme discomfort when in Black spaces because he was intensely aware of the lack of shared racially-informed culture. He remembers many instances during childhood and teen years that highlighted the racial difference between him and his parents, and he remembers the questions that arose from experiences in public and with family. How might we look accurately at the complexity present in terms of adjustment for this person? Measures such as those used in the studies referenced above would more than likely show that this participant possessed high levels of self-esteem, no behavioral problems, and good overall well-being. Yet, when we intentionally include his experiences and understandings of race, we see a normally invisible struggle just beneath the surface; one that will be with him throughout life.

Incorporating research focused on Black emerging adults, we must consider that this young man lived without a Black parent, which denied him a connection to someone with a shared racial identity with whom to discuss or show reactions to racial incidents rooted in life experience. Instead, he was raised by a White father who argued with him about who is to blame in police shootings of unarmed Black people. Similarly, for him and several other adoptees, they did not grow up hearing relatives discuss issues related to race and racism from the perspective of how to cope, survive, and gain individual and group resilience in the face of oppression. Instead, the perspective of Black people was often generally dismissed. Family exhibited discomfort related to seeing the role of White people in racial tension and violence, and they showed a lack of empathy regarding the personal significance of these events.

These factors are all "adjusted to" by adoptees. They find ways to cope, work to see the positives of their experience, fight for their racial identities, and continue bringing their voice and perspective. Perhaps sometimes they practice the understandable psychological defense of denial. However, can the additional arena of race be left out of measures of adjustment in transracial adoption and yield an accurate picture? The necessary adjustments are happening, and the help along the way found by participants are described in the subtheme, *Pathways, Influences, and Support*. Student organizations, mentors, peers, significant others: all of these help with the ongoing adjustment required of transracially adopted emerging adults on a daily basis.

In their narratives, adoptees described tension, awkwardness, discomfort, and fundamental disagreements related to issues of race with at least some of their family members. When family members are not taking it upon themselves to learn about race, their whiteness, and how racism affects Black, Indigenous, and People of Color, the onus for adjusting rests solely on the shoulders of adoptees. They must decide if and how to approach the subject of race, anticipate how the family member will react and how much energy the interaction will cost them, and they also deal internally with their own feelings about what is happening. Perhaps a better way to assess and measure adjustment within transracial adoptive families is to look at the extent to which families and adoptees adjust to being a multiracial family, what efforts are made by parents to question their own dominant racial identities in order to be able to have genuine interest in and compassion for the racial realities of their children, and attendance to adoptees' racial and adoptive identity development within the family.

Examining the level of support and comfort around communication related to race felt by adoptees within the family would help give a more accurate understanding of adjustment. This way, the responsibility for multiracial family adjustment would belong to the entire family system, rather than resting on adoptees alone. Understanding and assessing adjustment is more complicated than looking at measures of self-esteem, behavioral problems, and overall well-being. Within participant stories, we can see adjustment as a lifelong process intricately tied to issues of adoption, family, belonging, identity, and a collective social reality that makes race a primary factor.

Such research would potentially help guide training efforts for foster and adoptive parents, as well as bring attention to salient issues regarding racial identity for professionals involved with adoptive families such as teachers, counselors, social workers, and physicians. Perhaps most importantly, being clear about difficulties faced by adoptees provides support for greater investment in family preservation to decrease the disproportionate number of Black children and teens in foster care awaiting permanence. Ideally, future research would have three broad goals: (a) Raise awareness of race as a salient factor in foster care and adoption that needs to be addressed through improved training for TRA parents, and (b) Inspire improved systemic dynamics and investment in family preservation, and (c) include race and racial identity as factors in adjustment. In other words, help transracial adoption better meet the needs of Black adoptees and work systemically to decrease the number of children permanently removed from their birth families.

IMPLICATIONS FOR ADOPTIVE TRAINING AND POLICY

Current adoption policy requires that race not be considered in foster and adoptive placements. Because of this policy, many adoptive and foster agencies do not include mandatory multicultural trainings, and if they do voluntarily provide any training, they have no guidelines or standards for such trainings. Because of the practical link between policy and practice regarding training, the current study can provide evidence for important and needed changes in training and in policy.

Children and teens in care need support for permanence and also for valuing race as an important aspect of identity for both adoptee and adoptive parents. This goal could be met by requiring all foster and adoptive parents to complete a mandatory initial training and follow-up trainings that address race specifically. In those trainings, white privilege, whiteness, the racial history of transracial adoption, and research such as the current study could be included. Such a requirement would begin to sensitize parents to the importance of race, and illustrate that continuing to hold a strong white orientation is not conducive to ethically raising a child of a different race. The training should also focus on the formation of a truly multiracial family identity (Raible, 2006). This focus would call for training activities designed to present a multiracial family identity as beneficial for the entire family, not only the adopted child or children.

Advocacy for policy change by social workers, foster and adoptive parents, and all other professionals working with adoption is an important piece of this puzzle as well. Current policy that makes it possible for multicultural trainings to be optional and not standardized does not serve transracial adoptees. Several companies in the United States specialize in race-based trainings that teach the racial history of the country, the impact of racialization on Black, Indigenous, and People of Color and on White people, and ways to move toward anti-racism as an active identity development process. These companies could be consulted and contracted to provide comprehensive race-based training and to help organize follow-up activities for continued learning on the subject. A change to policy should be proposed, with the new policy stating that all foster and adoptive parents open to transracial placements must complete professionally facilitated race-based training as a part of the process.

IMPLICATIONS FOR COUNSELING PSYCHOLOGISTS

The results of this study provide some guidance for counseling psychology professionals, who may at some point work with adoptees of color from TRA families, TRA parents, or nonadopted siblings in counseling. The salience of race described by participants guides counseling professionals to bring race and identity into the counseling conversation by providing an invitation for transracially adopted clients to discuss experiences related to race in an affirming environment. Counseling psychology professionals should be ready to help adoptees explore their unique racial identity development process, to discuss wonderings about birth family, and to perhaps discuss ways to approach the topic of race with White parents. The results of this study suggest that adoptees want advocacy, compassionate listening from family members. They want family members to focus on gaining aware of issues related to race and identity, but they more often find these from peers and mentors. Counseling professionals can also provide some of this to clients who are transracially adopted. Of course, this calls for counseling professionals to live and develop a commitment to anti-racism and an understanding of systemic dynamics related to race.

When counseling families or White parents of TRA adoptees, this study suggests that helping the family system move toward a multiracial identity would be beneficial for each family member. This might include providing reading materials for parents and other family members and describing the importance of race and racial identity for everyone in the family. Pointing to the dynamics of race in the counseling room can add to the psychoeducation around race and racism. This can be done in an interpersonal process manner with compassion and guidance toward change and growth for White family members, with clear explanations of the inherited white racial frame and resulting systemic dynamics of privilege and oppression. Being aware of community resources for TRA families, such as anti-racism training or transracial adoption support groups, is another way that counseling psychologists can be of help. Counselors can help TRA parents and White adoptive siblings grow in the understanding that race is an important topic in the family and that growing in racial awareness and white anti-racist identity is vital in order to approach TRA effectively and ethically.

Appendix A

BOOK RECOMMENDATIONS

DiAngelo, Robin. *What Does it Mean to Be White: Developing White Racial Literacy*. New York: Peter Lang Publishing, 2016.

Feagin, Joe R. *The White Racial Frame: Centuries of Framing and Counter-Framing (2nd Ed.)*. New York: Routledge, 2013.

Hannah-Jones, Nikole, Roper, Caitlin, Silverman, Ilena, and Silverstein, Jake. *The 1619 Project: A New Origin Story.* First edition. New York: One World, 2021.

hooks, bell. *Writing Beyond Race: Living Theory and Practice*. New York: Routledge, 2012.

Kendi, Ibram X. *How to Be an Antiracist*. New York: One World, 2019.

Kendi, Ibram X. *How to Raise an Antiracist.* New York: One World, 2022.

Kendi, Ibram X. *The Antiracist Deck: 100 Meaningful Conversations on Power, Equity, and Justice*. New York: Clarkson Potter Publishers, 2022.

Reynolds, Jason and Kendi, Ibram X. *Stamped: Racism, Antiracism, and You*. New York: Little, Brown Books for Young Readers, 2020.

Roorda, Rhonda M. *In Their Voices: Black Americans on Transracial Adoption*. Columbia University Press, 2015.

Newton Verrier, Nancy. *The Primal Wound: Understanding the Adopted Child.* Baltimore, MD: Gateway Press, 1991.

Smith, Darron T., Jacobson, Cardell. K., and Juárez, Brenda G. *White Parents, Black Children: Experiencing Transracial Adoption*. Lanham, MD: Rowman & Littlefield Publishers, 2011.

Wilkerson, Isabel. *Caste: The Origins of Our Discontents*. New York: Random House, 2020.

FILM RECOMMENDATIONS

Adichie, Chimamanda Ngozi. *The Danger of a Single Story*. Filmed October 7, 2009 TED video. https://www.youtube.com/watch?v=D9Ihs241zeg&t=18s

Chon, Justin, dir. *Blue Bayou*. United States: Entertainment One, 2021

DuVernay, Ava, dir. *Colin in Black and White*. United States: Array Filmworks and Netflix, 2021

Tucker, Bryan, dir. *Closure: A Documentary about Adoption*. United States: Retrospect Productions, 2013.

Appendix B

DESCRIPTION OF CONCEPTS

Transracial adoption involves the intertwining of differing races and cultures, and thus intersects with the complex issues surrounding race (Kirton, 2000). Race, ethnicity, and culture are terms used to describe and categorize people. Racialization is a process that occurs when race is ascribed meaning in a society. Because of the layers of meaning associated with these words, and the different ways these words are used, my working understanding of these concepts in the current study is important to describe.

RACE

Race is a term with varying definitions and conceptualizations in academic literature. Baden and Steward (2007a) explain that race has been commonly understood as heritage with a group based on geography and a common set of physical characteristics such as skin color, hair texture/color, and facial features. However, Baden and Steward acknowledge that such a definition reifies race as though it has a biological basis, and so they refer to race as a social construction rather than a scientific classification. Kirton (2000) states that the existence of race in any scientific, biological or genetic sense has been widely discredited. Dennis (1995) explains that genetically, more variation is found among people of the same race than people of differing racial categories. Even while race does not have any genetic or biological basis, it is an important socially and legally constructed system of meaning in our society (Bonilla-Silva, 2014). This system affects identity formation and life experience (Samuels, 2009). In other words, for people of color, race is very real, because it is an idea that is widely shared, and this idea influences how people are treated. Even though there is no genetic basis for this societal reality of race, it is known as a real phenomenon, and, therefore, must be considered.

Black emerging adults are negotiating a world where a new rise in overt racism is creating new anxiety and tension for people of color in the United States. Since the 2012 shooting of Trayvon Martin in Florida, the shooting of Michael Brown in Ferguson at the hands of police, and a series of highly publicized incidents in which police shot and killed unarmed Black men, the Black Lives Matter movement began (Hall, Hall, Perry, & Kazak, 2016). The Black Lives Matter movement extends the work of previous civil rights movements, including the antilynching movement, that challenged forms of oppression that act on Black people (Nelson, 2016). Articles have arisen in peer-reviewed journals that attempt to understand police killings of Black people from a variety of perspectives and to offer support for Black men and families dealing with the trauma related to police violence against Black people (Aymar, 2016; Hall et al., 2016; Staggers-Hakim, 2016; Tolliver, Hadden, Snowden, Brown-Manning, 2016).

On the heels of this highly publicized violence against Black people, Donald Trump was elected President of the United States in 2016. Okeowo (2016) reports that since the election, a dramatic increase in overt racist and xenophobic acts of aggression and violence has been measured. The Southern Poverty Law Center (2016) reports that 437 incidents of intimidation (targeting Black people, immigrants, Muslim-Americans, people in the LGBT community, Jewish community centers, and women) were reported to them *between November eighth and fourteenth* directly following the election. Expanding these findings, 1091 incidents were reported between November eighth and December 12th. In the community in which I live, a parent at my daughter's school, who is a Black woman, came to school one morning visibly shaken and upset after she had been walking into a gas station that morning, and a White man in a big truck drove close to her and screamed, "It's Trump's America now, [N-word]."

While systemic racism has never been resolved in this country, the recent rise in overt incidents related to race and the publicizing of those incidents, is something that will be part of emerging Black adults' narratives. Not surprisingly, participants in the current study each mentioned the current racial climate and the racial politics in the US that affect them on a daily basis. This place in history calls for hermeneutic phenomenological inquiry to gain detailed descriptions of understandings of everyday experiences, no matter how seemingly inconsequential, to form a rich and textured picture of the phenomenon of emerging adulthood as a Black transracial adoptee who was raised by White parents.

RACIALIZATION

Racialization is a term that has been used in academic literature as an attempt to move further from the concept of race as a genetic reality, and, instead, switch attention to the processes through which ideas about race originate and develop historically (Kirton, 2000). Racialization is the act of making race appear real. Kirton cites the European racialization of Africans as the most powerful example of entire groups being racialized and treated collectively as a race. The historical roots and current effects of racialization are relevant within the topic of transracial adoption. As McRoy and Grape (1999) state, there are aspects of socially imposed racial categories that must be addressed: (a) differences in racial socialization experiences, (b) socially recognized phenotypical characteristics that cause people to classify other people as certain races, and (c) racial identity formation, or the process of coming to understand one's own identity as a person of a certain race, both personally and as part of a group. Kirton (2000) reminds us that we resist the consequence of racial thinking, and yet we are forced to accept its importance.

As Samuels (2009) states, the racialized social and political history of the United States is inextricably intertwined with the history of adoption in the United States. Indeed, Black children and their White parents cannot escape being racialized since their life stories take place within a racialized society. In the literature review that follows, a discussion of important historical events that have contributed to the complexities of transracial adoption is included.

ETHNICITY

Ethnicity is a term commonly referred to as a group of people sharing a common culture, religion, language or nationality (Hughes et al., 2006). Baden and Steward (2007a) state that ethnicity includes values, customs, and ancestry. Kirton (2000) describes ethnicity as pertaining to a shared common descent and cultural heritage (language, religion, customs, values, etc.). Some aspects of ethnicity can overlap with aspects of race and culture. Therefore, distinguishing racial, ethnic and cultural socialization can be confusing (Hughes et al., 2006).

Baden and Steward (2007a) point out some problems with the term ethnicity in relation to transracial adoption:

> Ethnicity bridges aspects of both race and culture, but does not allow for clear distinctions between them. Furthermore, use solely of the term ethnicity can be problematic given the ease with which individuals may choose to use the term ethnicity as an excuse to focus on the more familiar and less threatening

> concepts of culture and cultural activities as opposed to the very important, sometimes uncomfortable, and clearly socially constructed meanings that accompany race. (p. 93)

Baden and Steward (2007a) recommend the use of the terms race and culture in transracial adoption research, with the justification that these terms maintain the distinctions that they find vital to understanding the lived experience of transracial adoptees. In this way, the realities of a racialized world classifying people as belonging to certain racial groups, as well as personal cultural practices can be distinguished and included.

CULTURE

Culture is referred to as traditions, history, beliefs, practices, and values (Baden & Steward, 2007a). These are passed down over generations in both explicit and implicit ways. Culture has also been used in reference to expressions of tradition: festivals, food, rituals, or styles of dress. Culture is an important concept in relation to transracial adoption in that identities in transracial adoptees can be contradicting. For example, a transracially adopted child may have a phenotypical appearance consistent with a socially designated (and perhaps personally claimed) Black racial identity, but, because of the home, community, and school environments, might engage in cultural practices more consistent with a White cultural identity (Baden & Steward, 2007b). This points to Lee's (2003) assertion that transracial adoptees are seen as racial minorities in society but are sometimes perceived (by others and themselves) as members of majority culture due to adoption into a White family.

SYSTEMIC RACISM

Systemic racism refers to the foundational presence of racism within the United States; specifically, within its systems of government, economics, land ownership, housing, education, health care, criminal justice, and employment. The foundational presence of racism began with the intentional extermination and removal of people indigenous to North America and continued with the forced enslavement of Africans to be used as free labor in the United States (DiAngelo, 2016). These major components of United States history began an infusion of racialization and inequality into the laws and customs that formed the country, and they continue to be followed contemporarily. The existence of systemic racism causes racism to be a default presence in the United States (considered "normal"), overtly and implicitly affecting everyone through positions of hierarchical power based on skin color (Delgado & Stefancic, 2012). Systemic racism is described by Feagin (2010) as including a wide assortment of practices that are racist: (a) unjustly gained economic and political power of White people, (b) continuing resource inequalities, (c) the rationalizing White-racist frame, and (d) major institutions created to preserve White advantage and power.

White Racial Frame

The *white racial frame* (Feagin, 2010; 2013) is a model explaining and describing systemic racism. The white racial frame outlines the historical building blocks and lasting systemic constructs that maintain and perpetuate White supremacy and racism in United States culture. The white racial frame is a conditioned conceptual map that influences cognition and filters out ideas and experiences that do not fit (Smith, Jacobson, & Juárez, 2011). Feagin (2013) describes the white racial frame as an organized set of racialized ideas, stereotypes, emotions, and inclinations to discrimination that are passed down from generation to generation both explicitly and implicitly. This frame is especially persistent because it is embedded deeply in United States social structure. The white racial frame is recognizable across layers of society from the personal to the systemic. It includes individual bias, but it is also a multifaceted and multilayered system into which we are all born and socialized in the United States. For example, even if a person does not use racial slurs, that person is aware of the commonly and historically used racial slurs and negative stereotypes about different racial groups in the United States. This shows how even without explicit instruction, the white racial frame and the result of that frame are programmed into the minds of people. The unconscious influences are important to consider because White people in power are influenced by negative stereotypes held societally, and this influences hiring decisions, mortgage approvals, admissions choices, and other daily interactions that impact major life arenas.

Viewing transracial adoption within the context of the white racial frame and systemic racism, the controversy about transracial adoption can be seen as a byproduct of a systemically racist society. To see the systemic context, White people must engage in a critical examination of the racially oppressive society created by ancestors and perpetuated into contemporary times (Feagin, 2010). Because of the unique, historically rooted, dehumanizing racial framing of Black Americans that began with the enslavement of African people for labor in the North American colonies, the modern-day experiences of Black Americans are tied to that specific history and the framing used to justify slavery. Likewise, the modern-day experiences of White Americans are tied to the specific history and framing of White people as the "owners" of other human beings. Because of these unique historical facts, Black transracial adoptees should be considered as a unique population, and not grouped with other racial minorities. While all racial minorities are positioned below White people on the racial hierarchy in the United States, the Black experience in America is not the same as the Indigenous American, Latinx, Asian American, or Arab American experience. One can see that the disproportionate number of Black children in the foster care system awaiting adoption (Donaldson Adoption Institute, 2008; Lee, 2003) and the lack of recruitment of Black adoptive families (Donaldson Adoption Institute, 2008; McRoy & Griffin, 2012). Also, most foster care workers in charge of decisions about child removal and family preservation are White women (Barn, 2013). These facts reflect the racialized power differential that weaves through all United States institutions.

The theoretical lens of the white racial frame provides a structure to examine transracial adoption within the historically rooted social context in the United States. After all, if racism were not a primary social context in the United States, transracial adoption would not be a focus of study, research, and social inquiry. As Baden and Steward (2007a) remind us, transracial adoption has been referred to as cultural genocide by African American and American Indian organizations, and by developing countries from which White American people have adopted many children. The systemic lens acknowledges that we are all a product of a racialized society, and that the first step toward being able to transcend or alter that paradigm is to become aware of its constant and pervasive presence.

USE OF TERMS

In this book, focus will be placed on race and culture, as well as racial and cultural socialization. The choice to focus on these terms and concepts is related to the historical and theoretical links between transracial adoption, race, and culture in the United States. In this book, the term *White* will be used to refer to transracial adoptive parents who are of European/Caucasian descent, and the term *Black* will be used to refer to domestically adopted, US born, transracial adoptees who identify as Black, African American, or Biracial with Black parentage. Transracially adopted children may have several intersecting identities that are relevant to their development, and adoptive parents might also claim intersecting identities that affect parenting practices. However, racial and cultural identities will be the focus of this study. This focus is not meant to dismiss the presence of other possible identities, but to intentionally bring emphasis to issues centered on race and culture in transracial adoption. The term ethnicity will be avoided when possible, due to the potentially confusing overlap with race and culture described above. The term *racialized* will be used to describe the process of one's race becoming salient. For example, when a transracial adoptee experiences being negatively stereotyped as a Black person in the United States, they are experiencing racialization; their race is suddenly an important factor in the situation.

References

Adichie, Chimamanda Ngozi. "The Danger of a Single Story." Filmed October 7, 2009 TED video. https://www.youtube.com/watch?v=D9Ihs241zeg&t=18s

Alexander, R. Jr., and Curtis, C. M. "A Review of Empirical Research Involving the Transracial Adoption of African American Children." *Journal of Black Psychology* 22 (May, 1996): 223–235. https://doi.org/10.1177 percent2F00957984960222007

Andujo, E. "Ethnic Identity of Transethnically Adopted Hispanic Adolescents." *Social Work* 33, no. 6 (November-December,1988): 531–535. https://doi.org/10.1093/sw/33.6.531

Aymer, S. R. "'I Can't Breathe': A Case Study—Helping Black Men Cope with Race-Related Trauma Stemming from Police Killing and Brutality." *Journal of Human Behavior in the Social Environment* 26, no. 3–4 (2016): 367–376. DOI: 10.1080/10911359.2015.1132828

Baden, Amanda. "The Psychological Adjustment of Transracial Adoptees: An Application of the Cultural-Racial Identity Model." *Journal of Social Distress and the Homeless* 11, no.2. (2002): 167–191. doi: 10.1023/A:1014316018637

Baden, Amanda. L., and Steward, Robbie. J. "The Cultural-Racial Identity Model: A Theoretical Framework for Studying Transracial Adoptees." In *Handbook of Adoption: Implications for Researchers, Practitioners, And Families* edited by R. A. Javier, A. L. Baden, F. A. Biafora, A. Camancho-Gingerich (pp. 90–112). Thousand Oaks, CA: Sage Publications, Inc., 2007a.

Baden, Amanda. L., and Steward, Robbie. J. "Identity, Psychological Adjustment, Culture, and Race: Issues for Transracial Adoptees and the Cultural-Racial Identity Model." In *Handbook of Adoption: Implications For Researchers, Practitioners, And Families,* edited by R. A. Javier, A. L. Baden, F. A. Biafora, A. Camancho-Gingerich (pp. 359–377). Thousand Oaks, CA: Sage Publications, Inc., 2007b.

Barn, Ravinder. "'Doing the Right Thing': Transracial Adoption in the USA." *Ethnic and Racial Studies* 36, no. 8, (May, 2013): 1273–1291. doi: 10.1080/01419870.2013.770543

Bauermeister, J. A., Meanley, S., Hickok, A., Pingel, E., and VanHemert, W. "Sexuality-Related Work Discrimination and its Association with the Health of

Sexual Minority Emerging and Young Adult Men in the Detroit Area." *Sexuality Research and Social Policy* 11, no.1 (2014): 1–10.

Benson, P. L., Sharma, A. R., and Roehlkepartain, E. C. *Growing up adopted*. Minneapolis, MN: Search Institute, 1994.

Bentley-Edwards, K., and Stevenson, H. "The Multidimensionality of Racial/Ethnic Socialization: Scale Construction for the Cultural and Racial Experiences of Socialization" (CARES). *Journal of Child and Family Studies* 25 (2016): 96–108. Doi: 10.1007/s10826-015-0214-7

Berbery, M., and O'Brien, K. "Predictors of White Adoptive Parents' Cultural and Racial Socialization Behaviors with their Asian Adopted Children." *Adoption Quarterly* 14 (2011): 284–304. doi: 10.1080/10926755.2011.628265

Bonilla-Silva, Eduardo. *Racism without Racists: Colorblind Racism and the Persistence of Racial Inequality in America* (4th Ed.). New York: Rowman and Littlefield Publishers, Inc., 2014.

Brown, Tony N., and Lesane-Brown, Chase. L. "Race Socialization Messages across Historical Time." *Social Psychology Quarterly* 69, no. 2 (2006): 201–213. doi: 10.1177/019027250606900205

Bumpus, Jennifer. "Transracial Adoption: Racial Identity, Resilience, and Self-Esteem of African American Adoptees." PhD diss., University of Connecticut, 2015.

Burrow, Anthony, and Finley, G. E. "Transracial, Same-Race Adoptions, and the Need for Multiple Measures of Adolescent Adjustment." *American Journal of Orthopsychiatry* 74, no. 4 (October, 2004): 577–583, DOI: 10.1037/0002-9432.74.4.577

Children's Bureau. (2021). Foster care statistics 2019. https://www.childwelfare.gov / pubPDFs

Clark, K. B., and Clark, M. P. Racial Identification and Preferences in Negro Children. In *Readings in Social Psychology*, edited by E. MacCoby, T. Newcomb, and E. Hartlet (pp. 98–114). New York: Holt, 1958.

Daniel, J. L. and Daniel, J. E. "African-American Childrearing: The Context of a Hot Stove." In *Communication,Rrace, and Family: Exploring Communication in Black, White and biracial families,* edited by T. J. Socha and R. C. Diggs (pp. 45–68). Mahwah, NJ: Erlbaum, 1999.

Delgado, R., and Stefancic, J. *Critical Race Theory: An Introduction* (2nd Ed.). New York: New York University Press, 2012.

DeBerry, Kimberly, Scarr, Sandra, and Weinberg, Richard. "Family Racial Socialization and Ecological Competence: Longitudinal Assessments of African-American Transracial Adoptees." *Child Development* 67, no. 5 (1996): 2375–2399. doi: 009-3920/96/6705-0013

Dennis, Rutledge M. "Social Darwinism, Scientific Racism, and the Metaphysics of Race." *The Journal of Negro Education* 64, no. 3 (Summer, 1995) 243–252.

DiAngelo, Robin. *What Does it Mean to Be White: Developing White Racial Literacy*. New York: Peter Lang Publishing, 2016.

Eldridge, Sherrie. *Twenty Things Adopted Kids Wish Their Adoptive Parents Knew*. UK: Delta Publishing, 1999.

Endicott, J., Spitzer, R. L., Fleiss, J. L., Cohen, J. "The Global Assessment Scale: A Procedure for Measuring Overall Severity of Psychiatric Disturbance." *Archival General Psychiatry* 33 no. 6 (June, 1976): 766–771. DOI:10.1001/archpsyc.1976.01770060086012

Englander, M. The Phenomenological Method in Qualitative Psychology and Psychiatry. *International Journal of Qualitative Studies on Health and Well-being* 11 (2016): 1–11. http://dx.doi.org/10.3402/qhw.v11.30682

Evan B Donaldson Institute. *Finding families for African American Children: The role of race and law in adoption from foster care*. New York: Evan B Donaldson Institute, 2008.

Feagin, Joe R. *Racist America. Roots, Current Realities, and Future Reparations (2nd ed.)*. New York: Routledge, 2010.

Feagin, Joe R. Foreword. In D. T. Smith, C. K. Jacobson, and B. G. Juarez (Authors), *White Parents, Black Children: Can White Parents Teach Adoptive Black Children How to Cope with Race and Racism?* (pp. vii–xii). Lanham, MD: Rowman and Littlefield Publishers, Inc., 2011.

Feagin, Joe R. *The White Racial Frame: Centuries of Framing and Counter-Framing (2nd Ed.)*. New York: Routledge, 2013.

Feigelman, William. "Adjustments of Transracially and Inracially Adopted Young Adults." *Child and Adolescent Social Work Journal* 17, no. 3 (June, 2000): 165–184. doi: 10.1023/A:1007531829378

Finlay, Linda. "Engaging Phenomenological Analysis." *Qualitative Research in Psychology* 11 (March, 2014): 121–141, https://doi.org/10.1080/14780887.2013.807899

Folaron, Gail and Hess, Ped McCartt. "Placement Considerations for Children of Mixed African American and Caucasian Parentage." *Child Welfare* 72, no. 2 (March/April, 1993): 113–125. doi: 0009-4021/93/020113-13

Giorgi, A. "The Descriptive Phenomenological Psychological Method." *Journal of Phenomenological Psychology* 43, no.1 (2012): 3–12.

Grotevant, H. D. "Coming to Terms with Adoption: The Construction of Identity from Adolescence into Adulthood." *Adoption Quarterly* 1, no.1 (1997), 3–27.

Grotevant, H. D., Dunbar, N., Kohler, J.K., and Esau, A. M. L. "Adoptive Identity: How Contexts within and Beyond the Family Shape Developmental Pathways." *Family Relations: Interdisciplinary Journal of Applied Family Studies,* 49, no. 4, (2000): 379–387.

Hagerman, M. A. "White Families and Race: Colour-Blind and Colour-Conscious Approaches to White Racial Socialization." *Ethnic and Racial Studies* 37, (2014): 2598–2614. doi: 10.1080/01419870.2013.848289

Hagerman, Margaret Ann. "White Racial Socialization: Progressive Fathers on Raising 'Antiracist' Children." *Journal of Marriage and Family* 79, no. 14 (October, 2017): 60–74. doi: 10.1111/jomf.12325

Hall, Alison. V., Hall, Erika V., and Perry, Jaimie L. "Black and Blue: Exploring Racial Bias and Law Enforcement in the Killings of Unarmed Black Male Civilians." *American Psychologist* 71, no. 3 (2016):175–186. https://doi/10.1037/a0040109

Hayes, Mellonie. "A Look at Black Ethnic Identity and Transracial Adoption: A Contextual Perspective." PhD diss., University of Florida, 2008.

Herman, Ellen. Kinship by Design: A History of Adoption in the Modern United States. Chicago, IL: University of Chicago Press, 2008.

Hollingsworth, Leslie D. "Effect of Transracial/Transethnic Adoption on Children's Racial and Ethnic Identity and Self-Esteem: A Meta-Analytic Review." *Marriage and Family Review* 25, no. 1–2 (1997): 99–13.

Hollingsworth, Leslie D. "Promoting Same-Race Adoption for Children of Color." *Social Work* 43, no.2 (March, 1998): 104–116.

hooks, bell. *Writing Beyond Race: Living Theory and Practice*. New York: Routledge, 2012.

Hope, Elan. C., Hoggard, Lori. S. and Thomas, Alvin. "Emerging into Adulthood in the Face of Racial Discrimination: Physiological, Psychological, and Sociopolitical Consequences for African American Youth." *Translational Issues in Psychological Science*, 1, no.4 (2015): 342–351.doi: http://dx.doi.org/10.1037/tps0000041

Hughes, Diane, and Chen, Lisa. "When and What Parents Tell Children about Race: An Examination of Race-Related Socialization among African American Families." *Applied Developmental Science,* 1, no. 4 (1997): 200–214. doi: 10.1207/s1532480xads01044

Hughes, Diane and Johnson, Deborah. "Correlates in Children's Experiences of Parents' Racial Socialization Behaviors." *Journal of Marriage and Family,* 63, no. 4 (March, 2004): 981–995. doi:10.1111/j.1741-3737.2001.00981.x

Hughes, Diane. "Correlates of African American and Latino Parents' Messages to Children about Ethnicity and Race: A Comparative Study of Racial Socialization." *American Journal of Community Psychology* 31, no. 1–2 (March, 2003): 15–33. doi: 0091-0562/03/0300-0015/0

Hughes, Diane., Rodriguez, James, Smith, Emilie. P., Johnson, Deborah. J., Stevenson, Howard. C., and Spicer, Paul, "Parents' Ethnic–Racial Socialization Practices: A Review of Research and Directions for Future Study." *Developmental Psychology* 42, no. 4 (September, 2006): 747–770. doi: 10.1037/0012-1649.42.5.747

Hurd, N. M., Sellers, R. M., Cogburn, C. E., Butler-Barnes, S. T., and Zimmerman, M. A. "Racial Identity and Depressive Symptoms among Black Emerging Adults: The Moderating Effects of Neighborhood Racial Composition." *Developmental Psychology*, 49, no. 5 (2013): 938–950. doi: 10.1037/a0028826

Jennings, P. "The Trouble with the Multiethnic Placement Act: An Empirical Look at Transracial Adoption." *Sociological Perspectives,* 49 (2006): 559–581.

Juffer, Femmie and van IJzendoorn, Marinus H. "Adoptees do not lack self-esteem: A meta-Analysis of studies on self-esteem of transracial international, and domestic adoptees." *Psychological Bulletin* 133, no. 6 (November, 2007): 1067–1083. doi: 10.1037/0033-2909.133.6.1067

Kirton, Derek, *'Race,' ethnicity, and adoption*. Philadelphia, PA: Open University Press, 2000.

Langrehr, Kimberly J., Thomas, Anita Jones, and Morgan, Sydney K. "Confirmatory Evidence for a Multidimensional Model of Racial-Ethnic Socialization for

Transracially Adoptive Families." *Cultural Diversity and Ethnic Minority Psychology* 1, no. 3 (July, 2016): 1–8. doi: 10.1037/cdp0000081

Lee, Richard M. "The Transracial Adoption Paradox: History, Research and Counseling Implications of Cultural Socialization." *The Counseling Psychologist* 31, no. 6 (2003): 711–744. doi: 10.1177/0011000003258087

Lee, Richard. M., Grotevant, Harold D., Hellerstedt, Wendy L., Gunnar, Megan R. "Cultural Socialization in Families with Internationally Adopted Children." *Journal of Family Psychology* 20, no. 4 (December, 2006): 571–580.

Lesane-Brown, Chase L. "Race Socialization in Black Families: A Selective Review of the Literature." *Developmental Review* 26, no. 4 (2006): 400–426. doi:10.1016/j.dr.2006.02.001

Leslie, Leigh A., Smith, Jocelyn R., Hrapczynski, Katie M., and Riley, Debbie. "Racial Socialization in Transracial Adoptive Families: Does It Help Adolescents Deal with Discrimination Stress?" *Family Relations* 62, no. 1 (January, 2013) 72 – 81. doi:10.1111/j.1741-3729.2012.00744.x

Massati, Richard R., Vonk, Elizabeth. M., and Gregoire, Thomas K. "Reliability and Validity of the Transracial Adoption Parenting Scale." *Research on Social Work Practice* 14, no. 1 (January, 2004): 43–50. doi: 10.1177/1049731503257807

McRoy, Ruth G., and Zurcher, L. A. *Transracial and Inracial Adoptees: The Adolescent Years*. Springfield, IL: Thomas, 1983.

McRoy, Ruth G. "An Organizational Dilemma: The Case of Transracial Adoptions." *The Journal of Applied Behavioral Science,* 25, no. 2 (May, 1989): 145–160.

McRoy, Ruth G., and Grape, Helen. "Skin Color in Transracial and Inracial Adoptive Placements: implications for special needs adoptions." *Child Welfare*, 78, (September, 1999): 673–692.

McRoy, Ruth. G., and Griffin, Amy. "Transracial Adoption Policies and Practices: The US Experience." *Adoption and Fostering,* 36, no. 3–4 (October, 2012): 38–49. https://doi.org/10.1177/030857591203600305

Munsey, Christopher. "Emerging adults: The In-Between Age." *Monitor on Psychology,* 37, no. 7 (June, 2006) 68. http://www.apa.org/monitor/jun06/emerging.aspx

National Association of Black Social Workers. "*Positional Statement on Trans-Racial Adoptions*." 1–4 (1972). Retrieved from: http://nabsw.org/?page=PositionStatements

Nelson, Alondra. "The Longue Durée of Black Lives Matter." *American Journal of Public Health,* 106, no.10 (September, 2016),1734–1737. doi: 10.2105/AJPH.2016.303422

NPR (January 26, 2014). "Growing Up 'White': Transracial Adoptee Learned to Be Black." Retrieved from http://www.npr.org/2014/01/26/266434175/growing-up-white-transracial-adoptee-learned-to-be-black

Newton Verrier, Nancy. *The Primal Wound: Understanding the Adopted Child.* Baltimore, MD: Gateway Press, 1991.

Okeowo, A. "Hate on the Rise After Trump's Election." November, 2016, *The New Yorker* (online edition), Retrieved from http://www.newyorker.com/news/news-desk/hate-on-the-rise-after-trumps-election.

Orbe, Mark P. “Communicating about ‘Race’ in Interracial Families.” In *Communication, Race, and Family: Exploring Communication in Black, White and Biracial Families,* edited by T. J. Socha and R. C. Diggs, (pp. 67–180). Mahwah, NJ: Erlbaum, 1999.

Orbe, Mark. P. (2000). “Centralizing Diverse Racial/Ethnic Voices in Scholarly Research: the Value of Phenomenological Inquiry.” *International Journal of Intercultural Relations* 24 (2000): 603–621.

Orbe, M. P., Harrison, R., Kaufmann, Lydia D., and Laurent, Vanessa. “Evolutions of Cultural Contractual Understanding: Exploring Biracial Women’s Communicative Experiences.” *Howard Journal of Communication* 26, no. 4 (October, 2015): 422–443. doi: http://dx.doi.org/10.1080/10646175.2015.1080638

Park, Shelley M., and Green, C. E. “Is Transracial Adoption in the Best Interests of Ethnic Minority Children?” *Adoption Quarterly* 3, no. 4 (June, 2000): 5–34. doi: 10.1300/J145v03n04_02

Patel, T. “Theorising the Racial Identity Development of Transracial Adoptees: A Symbolic Interactionist Perspective.” *Adoption and Fostering* 31, no. 2 (July, 2007): 2–43. DOI:10.1177/030857590703100207

Pew Research Center. “Millennials.” 2017, http://www.pewresearch.org/topics/millennials/

Raible, John. “Lifelong Impact, Enduring Need.” In *Outsiders Within: Writing on Transracial Adoption, e*dited by Sun Yung Shin, Chinyere Oparah, and Jane Jeong Trenka. 179–188. Boston: South End Press, 2006.

Reynolds, Jamila. E., Gonzales-Backen, Melinda A., Allen, Kimberly A., Hurley, Eric A., Donovan, Roxanne. A., Schwartz, Seth J., Hudson, Monkia, Agocha, Bede, and Williams, Michelle “Ethnic-Racial Identity of Black Emerging Adults: The Role of Parenting and Ethnic-Racial Socialization.” *Journal of Family Studies* 38, no 15 (February, 2016): 1–25. DOI: http://dx.doi.org/10.1177/0192513X16629181

Robinson, Fawn T. “The Unguided Journey: The Impact of Racial Oppression on the Career Development Process of African-American Emerging Adults” (PhD diss., Duquesne University, 2016.

Roorda, Rhonda M. *In Their Voices: Black Americans on Transracial Adoption.* Columbia University Press, 2015.

Samuels, Gina Miranda ““Being Raised by White People”: Navigating Racial Difference among Adopted Multiracial Adults.” *Journal of Marriage and Family* 71, no. 1 (February, 2009): 80–94. https://doi.org/10.1111/j.1741–3737.2008.00581.x

Shireman, Joan F., and Johnson, Penny R. “A Longitudinal Study of Black Adoptions: Single Parent, Transracial, and Traditional.” *Social Work 31*, no. 3 (May-June1986): 172–176. Retrieved from: http://www.jstor.org/stable/23713191

Simon, Rita and Alstein, Howard. *Transracial Adoptees and Their Families: A Study of Identity and Commitment*. New York: Praeger, 1987.

Simon, Rita. J., and Alstein, Howard. “The case for transracial adoption.” *Children and Youth Services Review* 18, no. 1–2 (1994): 5–22.

Smith, Darron T., Jacobson, Cardell. K., and Juárez, Brenda G. *White Parents, Black Children: Experiencing Transracial Adoption*. New York: Rowman and Littlefield Publishers, 2011.

Southern Poverty Law Center. "*Bias-Related Incidents in the Month Following the Election*." Retrieved from https://www.splcenter.org/hatewatch/2016/12/16/update-1094-bias-related-incidents-month-following-election, December 16, 2016.

Staggers-Hakim, Raja. "The Nation's Unprotected Children and the Ghost of Mike Brown, or the Impact of National Police Killings on the Health and Social Development of African American Boys." *Journal of Human Behavior in the Social Environment* 26, no. 3–4 (2016): 390–399. doi: 10.1080/10911359.2015.1132864.

Summers-Temple, Irene W. "Racial and Ethnic Socialization and Racial Identity in African American Emerging Adults Raised in Predominantly White Communities." PhD diss., 2012.

Taylor, Robert J. and Thornton, Michael C. "Child Welfare and Transracial Adoption." *Journal of Black Psychology* 22, no. 2 (1996): 282–291. doi: 10.1177/00957984960222016

Tolliver, Willie F. Hadden, B., Snowden, Fabienne, and Brown-Manning, Robyn. "Police Killings of Unarmed Black People: Centering Race and Racism in Human Behavior and the Social Environment Content." *Journal of Human Behavior in the Social Environment* 26, no. 3–4 (January, 2016): 279–286. https://doi.org/10.1080/10911359.2015.1125207

Tucker, Bryan. "Closure: A Documentary about Adoption [motion picture]." United States: Retrospect Productions, 2013.

Twine, France W., and Steinbugler, Amy. C. "The Gap Between Whites and Whiteness: Interracial Intimacy and Racial Literacy." *Du Bois Review* 3 (September, 2006): 341–363. doi: 10.10170S1742058X06060231

United States Department of Health and Human Services. "Recent Demographic Trends in Foster Care: Data Brief." *Office of Data, Analysis, Research and Evaluation*. Administration for Children and families, 2013.

Vittrup, Brigette. "Color Blind or Color Conscious? White American Mothers' Approaches to Racial Socialization." *Journal of Family Issues* 39, no. 3 (November, 2016): 1 –25 doi: 10.1177/0192513X16676858

Vonk, M. Elizabeth (2001). "Cultural Competence for Transracial Adoptive Parents." *Social Work* 46, no. 3 (July, 2001): 246–54. https://www.jstor.org/stable/23718649

Vonk, M. Elizabeth, and Angaran, Ruth. "Training for Transracial Adoptive Parents by Public and Private Adoption Agencies." *Adoption Quarterly* 6, no. 3 (September, 2002): 53–62. https://doi.org/10.1300/J145v06n03_04

Vroegh, Karen S. "Transracial Adoptees: Developmental Status After 17 Years." *American Journal of Orthopsychiatry* 67, no. 4 (1997): 568–575. doi: 10.1037/h0080254

White-Johnson, Rhonda L. "The Impact of Racial Socialization on the Academic Performance And Prosocial Involvement of Black Emerging Adults." *Journal of College Student Development* 56, no. 2 (March, 2015): 140–154.

Wilkerson, Isabel. *Caste: The Origins of Our Discontents*. New York: Random House, 2020.

Wilkerson, R. "The Racial Socialization Process of White Children." PhD diss., 2014.

Willis, M. G. "The Real Issues in Transracial Adoption: A Response." *Journal of Black Psychology* 22, no. 2 (1996): 246–253.

Woodcock, Anna, Hernandez, Paul R., Estrada, M., and Schultz, P. W. (2012). "The Consequences of Chronic Stereotype Threat: Domain Dis-Identification and Abandonment." *Journal of Personality and Social Psychology* 103 (July 2012): 635–646. DOI:10.1037/a0029120

Index

About the Author

Kyrai Antares, PhD, is a counseling psychologist and director of Find the Key Therapeutic and Consultation Services in Eugene, Oregon. Antares is a transracial adoptive parent and a white anti-racism consultant.

www.ingramcontent.com/pod-product-compliance
Ingram Content Group UK Ltd.
Pitfield, Milton Keynes, MK11 3LW, UK
UKHW041839031026
15587UKWH00002B/872

9 781666 914597